THE
EUMENIDES

BY **æSCHYLUS**

A Translation with Commentary by
HUGH LLOYD-JONES
Regius Professor of Greek
Oxford University

with a series introduction by Eric A. Havelock

PRENTICE-HALL, INC., ENGLEWOOD CLIFFS, N.J.

PRENTICE-HALL 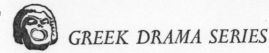 GREEK DRAMA SERIES

Series Editors

ERIC A. HAVELOCK, Sterling Professor of Classics, Yale University
MAYNARD MACK, Sterling Professor of English, Yale University

PA
3827
.E7
L5
1970
C2

8 82
A 8 0

90800
Nov. 1974

C13–291864–1
P13–291856–0

Library of Congress Catalog Card Number: 77–102282
Printed in the United States of America

Current Printing (last number):
10 9 8 7 6 5 4 3 2 1

PRENTICE-HALL INTERNATIONAL, INC. London
PRENTICE-HALL OF AUSTRALIA, PTY. LTD. Sydney
PRENTICE-HALL OF CANADA, LTD. Toronto
PRENTICE-HALL OF INDIA PRIVATE LIMITED New Delhi
PRENTICE-HALL OF JAPAN, INC. Tokyo

CONTENTS

FOREWORD TO THE SERIES

The Prentice-Hall Greek Drama Series will contain when completed the surviving tragedies of the Athenian stage. It offers each play in a separate inexpensive volume, so that readers may make their own personal selection rather than have the choice made for them, as is commonly the result when translations are issued in collective groups. It also offers each play in a context of exacting scholarship which seeks to make available to Greekless readers what the original Greek audiences responded to as they watched and listened to a performance. Under the English dress, in short, as far as humanly possible the Greek identity has been accentuated rather than obscured. Supported here by extensive introductions, notes, and appendices (in each case the work of an authority who has given painstaking attention to the full meanings of the text) and printed in a manner to exhibit their great varieties of formal structure, they step forth, untrammeled by preconceptions and conventional categorizations, as the highly individual creations they were when first performed.

The notes printed at the foot of each page to accompany the appropriate lines are in the first instance conceived as a corrective to shortcomings that no translation can avoid and should therefore be considered as in some sense an extension of the text. They testify to the fact that all translations in varying degree must indulge an element of deception, and they serve as a running attempt to explain its character and define its extent. In addition to this, they undertake to instruct the reader about conventions of idiom and imagery, of legend and allusion, which are native to the Greek situation and indispensable to a proper understanding of it. They aim also to get to the heart of the play as a work of art, exposing and explicating its often complex design in the hope that the reader thus aided will experience for himself its overwhelming dramatic effect.

M. M.

v

THE ATHENIAN DRAMATISTS

(Dates attested or probable are italicized)

AESCHYLUS	SOPHOCLES	EURIPIDES
525–456	*497/6–405/4*	*485/4–406/5*

AESCHYLUS	SOPHOCLES	EURIPIDES
Total production: c.90	Total production: c.125	Total production: c.92
Surviving plays: 7	Surviving plays: 7*	Surviving plays: 17*
First success *485*	First success *469*	First success *441*

AESCHYLUS	SOPHOCLES	EURIPIDES
The Persians 472		
The Seven Against Thebes 467		
The Suppliants 463?	*Ajax 460–45?* (date unknown— probably the earliest)	
Oresteia 458 (*Agamemnon, The Libation Bearers, The Eumenides*)	*Antigone 442–41*	
Prometheus Bound (date unknown probably late)	*The Women of Trachis* (date unknown)	*Alcestis 438* *Medea 431* *The Children of Heracles* c. *430–20*
	Oedipus the King 429–25?	*Hippolytus 428* *Hecuba* c. *425*
	Electra 420–10	*The Suppliants* c. 420 *Heracles* c. 420–16? *Andromache* c. 419 *Electra* c. *415–13* *The Trojan Women 415* *Helen 412* *Iphigeneia in Tauris* c. *412* *The Phoenician Women 410–9*
	Philoctetes 409	*Orestes 408* *Ion* c. 408? *The Bacchae* c. 406 (produced posthumously)
	Oedipus at Colonus c. *406–5* (produced posthumously)	*Iphigeneia at Aulis 406* (produced posthumously)

* disregarding *The Ichneutae* of Sophocles and *The Cyclops* and *Rhesus* of Euripides which are not tragedies.

INTRODUCTION TO THE SERIES

1. GREEK TRAGEDY TODAY

The table of the three tragedians and their productions facing this page reveals a situation which, judged by our experience of European drama since the Greeks, is, to say the least, unusual. The total of thirty-one plays was composed within a span of about sixty-five years, between 472 and 406 B.C., and that ends the story. It is as though the history of the English drama were confined to the Elizabethans and the Jacobeans and then closed. These thirty-one are survivors—a mere handful—of an originally enormous total. The three playwrights between them are credited with over three hundred titles, and the plays of their competitors, which except for isolated fragments and notices have now vanished from the record, are uncountable.

These facts shed light upon a familiar paradox: Classic Greek drama is at once parochial and universal, narrowly concentrated upon recurrent motifs, characters, and situations, yet always able to evoke a response at a level which is fundamental and general. Most of these hundreds of plays were composed in the years between the defeat of the Persians by the Greeks at Salamis in 480 B.C. and the defeat of Athens by Sparta in 404 B.C.; they were produced for audiences in Athens and in Attica, that small canton district which contains the city and is itself circumscribed by the sea and the mountains. The limits of history and geography surrounding them are therefore narrow and intense. Greek tragedy is Attic and Athenian not accidentally but essentially, and this fact cannot but have had strong influence in the dramatic choices made by the playwrights as they selected situation, theme, and characters. The vast bulk of the lost productions, had it been preserved, would, one suspects, retain interest today mainly for specialists and antiquarians. There is indeed a good deal of antiquarianism in the plays we do have. But they are products of their authors' maturity, none composed at an age earlier than forty-five. Their preservation, if we except a few plays of Euripides, reflects some value judgments passed in antiquity; they were on the whole better able to withstand changes of taste and fashion and shifts in the character and nationality of audiences and critics.

The present age has come to recognize a new-found affinity with them. During the last century and the early part of the present one, when study of the classics was still dominant in education, Greek drama was read and esteemed as an exercise in the grand style, a mirror of the eternal verities and familiar moral imperatives. Even Euripides, the least tractable of the three from the moral standpoint, was credited with a desire to set the world right. By and large, the watchword the Victorians heard in the plays was not danger but decorum. Today, a generation which has known frustration and disillusionment—desperately demanding some private identity within a society which seems imprisoned and perhaps doomed by its own prior commitments—can view these plays with clearer eyes for what they are: portrayals of the human dilemma which foreswear the luxury of moral confidence and assured solutions. Here are sufferings disproportionate to the original error, characters caught and trapped in situations which are too much for them and for which they are only partly responsible. Here are pity and terror treated as facts of life with which one must come to terms. Here finally is defiance combined with a fatalism which accepts the tragic scene even at the moment of its repudiation. The watchword we listen to today is not decorum but danger. For the children of men who now inherit the earth it is therefore possible to respond to the classic tragedy of the Greeks with a directness denied to the more secure temper of their forebears.

Translators of Greek drama face a difficult choice between editing the Greek into language which will appeal to the modern sensibility, or offering a version which attempts as close an approximation as possible to the form and content of the original. The present series has been conceived on the assumption that since form and content hang together, the one cannot be paraphrased without damaging the other. The damage usually is done by suppressing those features of the original which affront the modern sensibility, while exaggerating those that do not. Quite commonly the operatic form of the plays is in a modern version played down or even ignored, and the temptation is always strong so to interpret the plots as to center interest upon characters at the expense of situation. The versions offered in this series, while modest in their pretensions, have sought to maintain fidelity to that original convention of the Greek which divided the diction of a play between choric and lyric portions on the one hand and spoken dialogue on the other. The two together constituted the total dramatic statement, which was thus partly sung and partly recited, and they are here printed in different typefaces to bring out more clearly the way in which the play's structure is articulated. Passages in hexameters, anapests, and trochaic tetrameters were either sung or chanted, and accordingly are printed here as lyric. The notes also make some attempt to indicate the metrical arrangements practiced in the lyric portions and the emotional effects produced. To transfer these effects in translation from an inflected tongue quantitatively scanned is impossible, and the aids offered are therefore directed to the imagination of the reader rather than to his ear.

2. THE DRAMATISTS

The alienation of the artist is not a condition which the Greeks of the classical age would readily have understood. The three Greek tragedians were Attic born and men of their time, participating, as the record indicates, in the political and social life of their community. Their plays accordingly expose, examine, and question the values of Greek society, but they do not reformulate and they do not reject. This being said, one must add that differences of style and approach between them are marked. The grandiloquence of Aeschylus becomes an appropriate instrument for expressing the confident ethos of the Athenian democracy and a theology which would justify the ways of Zeus to men. In the more stringent style of Sophocles, the tragic hero and heroine endure an exposure which is often ironic but which penetrates to the core of their dilemma, while their essential dignity is preserved and even enhanced. Euripides, the "most tragic" of the three, comes nearest to stepping outside his society. His later plays in particular tend to place the traditional norms of heroic and aristocratic leadership in an equivocal light. But his plots, as they enlarge the roles of women, children, servants, and slaves, remain faithful also to the changing mores and manners which increasingly foreshadowed the individualism of the Hellenistic age.

AESCHYLUS was born c. 525–24 at Eleusis near Athens of an aristocratic family (*eupatrid*). At thirty-five he fought at Marathon, where his brother fell gloriously; he may have also fought at Salamis. He paid two visits to the court of Hieron in Sicily, who was the patron likewise of Pindar, Bacchylides, and

Simonides. At the first visit he composed a play for the court celebrating Hieron's founding of the new city of Aetna (after 476); the second visit was terminated by his death at Gela in his seventieth year (456), where an epitaph on his monument celebrated his service at Marathon. An Athenian decree subsequently provided for the revival of any of his plays at public expense. Though he was preceded in the composition of tragic drama by the semi-legendary Thespis, Aeschylus is for practical purposes the "founder" of this unique art form, combining choric performance with a plot supported by dialogue between two, later three, actors. He was both composer and actor-manager, taking leads himself in some of his plays, probably the early ones. He is credited with developing the conventions of grandiloquent diction, rich costuming, formal dance figures, and some degree of spectacular effect. Although he died only about fifty years before *The Frogs* appeared, by Aristophanes' day his life was already a legend. Later stories about him (e.g., that he was an "initiate" who betrayed the secret of the Mysteries, or that he retired to Sicily in discomfiture for a variety of alleged reasons) are probably the inventions of an age more biographically inclined than his own.

SOPHOCLES was born c. 496 of an affluent family at Colonus near Athens. Known for his good looks, he was also an accomplished dancer and lyre player who, at age sixteen, was selected to lead the paean of victory after Salamis. He was taught by Lamprus, a famous master of the traditional music. He played roles in some of his own early productions, but later desisted, because of his weak voice. He took considerable part in public life. In 443–42 he was imperial treasurer; he was elected general twice—once in 440, the year in which Pericles suppressed the revolt of Samos, and again at a later date as colleague of Nicias; also, in 413, when he was over eighty years old, he was appointed one of the special commissioners (*probouloi*) to review the aftermath of the Sicilian disaster. He held a lay priesthood in the cult of a local deity of healing and allowed his own house to serve as a shrine of Asclepius pending the completion of a temple. He founded an Association (*thiasos*) of the Muses (something like a literary club). Polygnotus painted a portrait of him holding the lyre, which was hung in the picture gallery on the Acropolis. Tradition connects him with prominent men of letters, such as Ion of Chios, Herodotus (there are discernible points of contact between the History and the plays), and Archelaus the philosopher. In 406 he mourned the death of his younger contemporary Euripides in a public appearance with actors and chorus at the rehearsal (*proagon*) for the Great Dionysia. Some months later he died, at the age of ninety. He was remembered and celebrated as an example of the fortunate life, genial, accomplished, and serene.

EURIPIDES was born c. 485 at Phyla in Attica, probably of a good family. He made his home in Salamis, probably on an estate of his father, where it is said he composed in a cave by the sea. He held a lay priesthood in the cult of Zeus at his birthplace. Tradition, supported by hints in Old Comedy and the internal evidence of his own plays, connects him with the leading sophistic and philosophical circles of the day: Anaxagoras, Archelaus, Prodicus, Protagoras, and above all Socrates, said to be an admirer of his plays. In musical composition, he was assisted by a certain Cephisophon; this collaboration was probably a common practice. He served on an embassy to Syracuse (date unknown) and composed a public elegy in 413 for the Athenian soldiers fallen in Sicily. Prisoners in the quarries are said to have won release from their captors by reciting his choruses. He appears to have preferred a life of some seclusion, surrounded by his household. In 408–7 he left Athens for the north. He stayed initially at Magnesia in Thessaly, where he was received with honors, and then at the court of Archelaus of Macedon. There, in addition to a court play composed in the king's honor, he produced *The Bacchae*, his last extant work. He died there in 406. Buried in Macedonia he was memorialized by a cenotaph at Athens. Some of his plays were produced posthumously by one of his three sons. A good deal of the tradition surrounding his parentage, domestic life, personal character, and contemporary reputation in Athens is unfriendly to him; but it is also unreliable, depending as it probably does on the satirical treatment which he often received from the comic poets.

3. THE TIMES

In 525, when Aeschylus was born, the "tyranny" established at Athens under Pisistratus and his sons was still in power. When he was five years old, the tyrants were expelled, and a series of constitutional changes began which were to result in the establishment of complete democracy.

Abroad, the Persian Empire, founded by Cyrus the Great, had already absorbed all of Asia Minor and extended its sway over the Ionian Greeks. The year of Aeschylus' birth had been marked by the Persian conquest of Egypt, followed by that of Babylon. When he was sixteen, the Ionian Greeks revolted against their Persian masters, were defeated and partially enslaved (494), after which the Persian power sought to extend its conquests to the Greek mainland. This attempt, repulsed at Marathon (490), was finally defeated at Salamis, Plataea, and Mycale (480–79). The Greeks in turn, under the leadership of Athens, liberated the Ionians from Persian control and established the Confederacy of Delos to preserve the liberty thus gained.

By degrees, this alliance was transformed into the Athenian Empire, governed by an ascendant and confident democracy, under the leadership of many eminent men, none more so than Pericles, whose political power lasted from about 460 to his death in 429. The empire, though supported as a defense against Persia, became the natural target of disaffected allies, who found themselves becoming subjects, and of the jealousy of other Greek states, notably Sparta and Corinth. In 432 a Peloponnesian coalition under Spartan leadership opened hostilities with Athens, ostensibly to free Greece from her yoke. The war lasted, with an interval of armistice, till 404, when Athens, exhausted and overextended by commitments, lost her last naval protection and was beseiged and captured by the Peloponnesian forces.

Within the two years preceding this event, Euripides and Sophocles had both died. The works of the three dramatists were therefore composed during an expansive age in which democracy at home was matched by imperialism abroad. The repulse of the foreign invader was followed by the extension of Athenian commerce and influence throughout the eastern Mediterranean, and to some extent in the west also. This brought in the revenues and also encouraged the confidence in leadership which supported Pericles' ambitious policies and adorned the Acropolis with those public buildings, unmatched in purity of style, which still stand there.

But before the last plays were written, the strain of an exhausting and demoralizing war with fellow Greeks was beginning to tell, and in a moment of crisis even the democratic constitution had been called in question (411). For Aeschylus, his city's history had been an unbroken success story. In the lifetime of his two successors, she confronted an increasing series of problems, military, political, and social, which proved too much even for her energies to sustain.

4. GREEK THEATRICAL PERFORMANCE

The twelfth chapter of Aristotle's *Poetics* contains the following statement:

. . . The quantitative sections . . . into which a tragedy is divided are the following: *prologos, epeisodion, exodos,* and the choral part, itself subdivided into *parodos* and *stasima.* These occur in all tragedies; there may also be actors' songs and *kommoi.*

The *prologos* is that whole section which precedes the entrance of the chorus; the *epeisodion* is a whole section between complete choral odes; the *exodos* is that whole section of a tragedy which is not followed by a choral ode. In the choral part, the entrance song (*parodos*) is the first complete statement of the chorus, a *stasimon* is a song of the chorus without anapests or trochees; a *kommos* is a dirge in which actors and chorus join. . . .*

Students in English literature and other fields are likely to have been introduced to this famous passage. Yet scarcely any statement about Greek drama has caused more misunderstanding. It is schematic when it should be tentative, and definitive when it should be approximate. It has encouraged the presumption, widely held, that Greek plays were constructed according to a standard model from which, to be sure, the dramatist might diverge on occasion, but which nevertheless was his model: A prologue was followed by a choric entrance, for which anapests were supposedly the normal vehicle, and this by dialogue divided into episodes separated by full choruses, and concluded by an exit after the last chorus. No doubt the anonymous author (Aristotle could scarcely have been so dogmatic or so wrong) reflects those standards of mechanical formalism current in the period of the drama's decline. The key statement, "These occur in all tragedies," is false. The suggestion that actors' songs and *kommoi* (duets, trios, and quartets) were additions to the standard form is equally false. In Aeschylus alone, the reader will discover that neither his *The Persians* nor his *The Suppliants* has either *prologos* or *exodos* (applying these terms as defined in the *Poetics*). If the *Prometheus Bound* has a *parodos*, it is technically a *kommos,* that is, a duet shared between Prometheus and the chorus. Two of the *stasima,* or choric odes, in *The Eumenides* are interrupted by nonchoric iambics. It would be interesting to know how the author of these remarks would apply his definition of *exodos* to *Agamemnon.* On his terms, the exodos extends from lines 1035 to 1673, but it includes one elaborate lyric duet sung by Cassandra and chorus, then the murder of Agamemnon, then an equally elaborate duet sung by Clytemnestra and chorus. The *parodos* of *The Seven Against Thebes* is not in anapests, nor is that of *The Eumenides,* and the *exodos* of *The Eumenides* is, in effect, an elaborate lyric trio shared between Athena and two different choruses.

No doubt the practice of Sophocles encouraged schematization, but even his practice often included in the *exodos* the climactic portions of the drama. *Oedipus the King* is an example. The practice of Euripides often reverts to the fluidity characteristic of Aeschylus. The fact seems to be that the whole conception of a tragedy as consisting of quantitative parts is erroneous, and the reader

---

* Translation by G. M. A. Grube, from *Aristotle on Poetry and Style.* New York: Liberal Arts Press, 1958.

is best advised to approach each play as, in some sense, a new creation. Hence, though translators in this series may from time to time use the classic, or neo-classic, terms of the *Poetics*, they may equally be forced to apply modern terminology and speak of choric or lyric songs, of acts and scenes, of entrances, exits, and finales, according as the specific structure of any given play may require.

The conditions of production have never since been duplicated, and since they affect the way the plays were written, a word about them is in order. Performances took place in the open air. The audience sat on benches inserted into the slope of a recessed hillside. Chorus and actors shared not a stage but a circular dancing floor, on which the audience looked down. Thus, the Greek play remained a spectacle for the eye, as well as a verbal and musical delight to the ear, particularly as the figures executed in the dances produced patterns which an elevated angle of vision could appreciate. The audience was rarely asked to imagine the action as taking place in a closed room. Forecourts and courtyards and the street itself predominate as settings under the Mediterranean sky, and that sky itself, as the reader will discover, is never very far away from the characters' thought and speech.

At the back of the dancing floor stood a temporary wooden structure, the proscenium, with a central and two side doors and a flat roof. The doors were used for entrances and exits, the roof as a platform for appearances that called for an elevated position (those of gods, and sometimes human beings like the Watchman in the opening scene of *Agamemnon*). Behind the proscenium the actors could change their costumes, which were formalized to indicate sex, age, and social status. It is important to distinguish the *characters* who appear in a given play from the *actors* who played their parts. The former, while few by Shakespearean standards, considerably outnumbered the latter, who were rationed to two in some plays, three in most (four occasionally and doubtfully). The practical effect was that not more than two or three speaking parts could be carried on at any one time, so that at least some of the characters had to be played by different actors at different times, and the actors, relying on costume changes, had to be prepared to change their roles with rapidity. This ancient convention had an important result: The personality of the actor was severed from the role he played—this was also an effect of his mask—and reduced in importance (that is, until conventions changed in the Hellenistic age); and hence the burden of dramatic emphasis had to be carried entirely by the language, whoever happened to be speaking it. This is one reason why the verbal virtuosity of Greek tragedy has never been surpassed, even by Shakespeare.

The limitation of actors to two or three was undoubtedly related to a practical necessity. To examine (as one can do very easily in the typography employed in this series) the proportions of lyric to dialogue in a Greek play—that is, of sung to spoken parts, as these are assigned to individual actors (ignoring the chorus)—is to discover that the actors, and not just the chorus, had to have excellent singing voices enabling them to sustain solos, duets, trios and quartets. Even if they were assigned on a trial basis—the precise details of selection are disputable—the supply of suitable voices would be limited, and would require rationing among several plays competing simultaneously.

The standard phrase to describe authorship was "to teach a chorus," while "to grant a chorus" indicated the procedures of acceptance which put a play in production. Both seem to argue for the priority of the chorus in the classic Greek conception though the degree of priority is again a matter of dispute. The assembling and training of a group of singers and dancers (the total number is in dispute and may have varied) obviously took the most time, money, and skill.

The expense was borne partly by the state and partly by private patrons, though the arrangements changed somewhat in the course of time. The playwright became his own producer, exercising a degree of control which is reflected in the tight unity of most Greek plays, exhibiting as they do something of the symmetry of Greek architecture.

The lyrics were accompanied by woodwinds, and the anapests, trochaic tetrameters, and dactyls were chanted, very possibly to the accompaniment of strings. The term chorus, however, indicates not singers but dancers, just as the terms strophe and antistrophe (which are Hellenistic), attached to symmetrical stanzas, originally indicated the turns and counter-turns of symmetrical dance patterns. This reminds us that, besides the music, we have lost the choreography, which was executed in figures of varying complexity. Conventions which today we would assign to ballet, opera, and oratorio are in Greek drama combined with a series of speaking parts to make something that we call by analogy a stage play, but which in fact is an ensemble uniquely Greek and classical and somewhat alien to modern expectations. It is a mistake, as any reader of *Agamemnon* or *Hippolytus* will discover, to think of plot as being restricted to the speaking parts. Lyric and dialogue are partners in the task of forwarding the action and exposing character and motive.

Though the place of performance of most but not all of these plays was the Theater of Dionysus on the southeast slope of the Acropolis and though one major occasion for the competition was the festival of the City Dionysia, this connection with the god and his cult—contrary to some widely held opinion—seems to have left no perceptible mark on the plays we have. *The Bacchae*, which might appear to be an exception, was not composed originally for performance in Athens, and its setting, we should note, is Theban. Even the Theater of Dionysus itself had replaced a more primitive arrangement in the market place. Furthermore tragic competitions were not restricted to the Dionysia. Latterly at least, they were also offered at the spring festival of the Lenaea. The link between Dionysus and the Greek theater became intimate in the Hellenistic age; their relationship in the sixth and fifth centuries is a matter of dispute, and was possibly somewhat fortuitous. Three prizes were awarded for first, second, and third places, and though special judges were selected for this purpose, they made their decision in front of the audience, which did not hesitate to register its own preferences. Thus the plays were composed for the Athenian public, not for an esoteric minority. Appeals to contemporary feeling on political and social issues are certainly not to be excluded on a priori grounds as violating the purity of Greek art. The reader himself will note without learned assistance how frequently a plot or episode manages to exploit Athenian pride and patriotism.

These original conditions of performance, as we have said, helped to mould the character of the text. The simplicity of the early playing area prompted the use of "verbal scenery" (instead of props and physical effects) and a "program" of plot and characters incorporated in the diction, most of it in the "prologue." But the plays were then revived continuously for centuries, during which time the details of staging, costumes, masks, the formal rules of dramaturgy, the profession of acting, and the construction of the theater itself, were all elaborated and formalized, even to some extent "modernized." The reader should be warned that in current handbooks on the subject he is likely to encounter much which draws on testimonies from these later periods, and which cannot be authenticated for the simpler but more creative conditions of the fifth century B.C.

E. A. H.

ON THE METRES OF GREEK TRAGEDY

One difference between Attic tragedy and opera is the domination of words over music. The music was there, in the choral passages, perhaps in all passages other than pure dialogue. But the rhythm of the words controlled the music. This is clearly to be inferred from the *strophic* structure of the full choral ode. A *strophe*, an elaborate series of metric elements arranged in a complex and unique pattern, will be followed by an *antistrophe* which repeats that pattern precisely, a long syllable in the one will match a long syllable in the other, and a short will match a short. This would be unthinkable as much in modern operatic forms as in medieval chant, where syllables can be lengthened or shortened, or can receive varying stress, as the rhythm of the music requires.

Greek metre depends on an alternation of long and short syllables, and not, as in English verse, on a sequence of stressed and unstressed syllables. In the main, there were three types of metre. First, in the dialogue, and in such passages as the spoken prologue and messengers' speeches, we have an iambic metre probably unaccompanied by music. It is called iambic trimeter because it can be best analyzed into three dipodies of two iambs each. There is a good analogy here with English blank verse, although the Greek line had six iambs rather than five as in English, and although the Greek line was stricter than the English analogue; in Greek comedy a good reader can instantly pick out a quoted or a parodied tragic trimeter from the surrounding comic trimeters by the greater regularity of the former. A typical line is 1. 12 of *Oedipus the King:*

ho pasi kleinos Oidipus kalumenos
the famous man whom all men know as Oedipus

where the single vertical represents the metrical division into dipodies, the double vertical the regular *caesura,* or word-ending within the third or fourth iambic foot.

When the chorus enter the orchestra in the *parodos,* again when they leave in the *exodos,* and in other passages, such as the introduction of new characters after a choral ode, the chorus, or one of the main characters, often speak in anapests. This metre can be arranged in lines, but in fact falls into *systems,* or long sequences, since there is no real metrical break at the end of the conventionally arranged lines. The series of anapests, that is, simply goes on until a shortened foot, a single syllable, coinciding with a verse-pause, ends the *system.* Thus we get ⌣ ⌣ − ⌣ ⌣ − . . . . ⌣ ⌣ − −. This is clearly a marching rhythm, and was usually accompanied by linear movement (on or off stage) by chorus or actors. Though some variations are allowed, spondees (− −) or dactyls (− ⌣ ⌣) sometimes replacing the anapests (e.g., ⌣ ⌣ − | − − | ⌣ ⌣ − | ⌣ ⌣ | ⌣ ⌣ − , etc. is possible), the anapestic is the steadiest, most driving, metre in Greek drama. Musically, it was probably between dialogue and choral song,

xiv

ON THE METRES OF GREEK TRAGEDY

probably accompanied by a simple melody and chanted rather than spoken, in a manner somewhat like *recitative*.

The full choral ode is an elaborate metrical, musical, and choreographic structure. In a modern English text, these odes often look like what used to be called *free verse*. They are in fact extremely tight structures, as the correspondence between strophe and antistrophe reveals. They are like free verse only in that each ode is a metrically unique creation: The metres are made up of known elements, but these elements are arranged into a pattern peculiar to the single ode.

The metrical structure of choral odes requires a book for adequate description. But three common types of metrical elements in them can be noted here. First *iambic*: here we have usually varied and syncopated iambic forms, appearing as short metrical cola, or sections; for example,

$$\smile - \smile - \mid \wedge - \smile - \mid \smile - \wedge -$$
$$\smile - \smile - \mid \wedge - \smile - \mid \smile - \wedge -$$

where the caret shows the missing syllable which would have made each of the three parts of these two cola (appearing as *lines* in our text) a standard iambic dipody. This metre is crisp and lively and relatively uncomplicated. In origin, it is closer to speech than other choral metres: In the hands of Aeschylus, it could reach (as in the choral odes of *Agamemnon*) an unparalleled religious and dramatic solemnity.

The favorite choral metre of Sophocles was the Aeolic (so-called because it appears in the lyric poetry of the Aeolic poets Sappho and Alcaeus) composed of elements which appear to be expanded choriambs ($-\smile\smile-$) with various combinations preceding and following them. The most common element is the glyconic $-\smile-\smile\smile-\smile-$; but endless variations are possible. It is perhaps the most mellifluous, and the most capable of subtle modulation of all choral metres. Sometimes iambic elements, and these sometimes in the form of a series of short syllables, will be introduced with great dramatic effect in an Aeolic sequence; and sometimes the Aeolic metre will be turned to the rapid and epic movement of a dactylic sequence ($-\smile\smile-\smile\smile\ldots$). Both these variations occur, for example, in the great first stasimon of *Antigone* (332 f.).

The wildest and most eccentric metre is the *dochmiac*, which seems to consist of staccato and abruptly syncopated iambic elements, typical forms being $\smile--\smile-$ and $\smile\smile\smile\ \smile\smile\smile-$. This metre is used to mark statements of great fear or grief. The *parodos* of *The Seven Against Thebes*, where the Theban women imagine their city taken, is an extended passage in dochmiacs. Another example is *Hippolytus*, 811 f., where the chorus lament the suicide of Phaedra. Here as often in dochmiac, lines of iambic trimeter, as in spoken dialogue, are interspersed (813, 819–28, etc.). This may correspond to a break in the music and dancing, a further dramatic representation of extreme anxiety.

These choral or sung metres are most often uttered by the chorus, but sometimes by a single character, in a monody, or more often, in a lyric dialogue with the chorus. This latter is called a *kommos*, literally (*self-*) *striking* or *lamentation*, because that is the usual mode of such passages. By its nature, the kommos is often in dochmiac metre.

These are three of the principal metrical forms in choral song. Each has its distinct *ethos*, or emotional tone; and this distinct emotion was elaborated and enhanced by the dancing as well as the music, both these parts of the overwhelming choral performance being composed so as to correspond to the metrical pattern.

Sometimes more special metres are used in choruses for more special effect, and we shall mention only two: (1) The chorus at the beginning of *Agamemnon* as they move from their marching anapests into song begin with a dactylic hexameter $-\smile\smile-\smile\smile-\smile\smile-\smile\smile--$, the metre of Homeric epic: that is clearly a deliberate recalling of the Homeric situation; (2) much of the *parodos* of *The Bacchae* (e.g., 64 ff.) is in an Ionic metre $\smile\smile--\smile\smile--$, etc. That is because this metre was used in ritual hymns to Dionysus.

Finally, we should note the trochaic tetrameter $-\smile-\smile\ \ -\smile-\smile\ \ -\smile-\smile$ $-\smile-$. A rapid and slightly rollicking form, this was said to be the original dialogue metre of tragedy, and its relative frequency in the early plays of Aeschylus may bear this out. It is a dialogue metre, is more formal than iambic trimeter, and expresses more hurry and agitation: e.g., *The Persians* 155–75, 215–48, where we note that for the Queen's long speech in 176–214, the metre reverts to the more conversational iambic trimeter.

The preceding is only a bare sketch of the intricacies, as well as the expressive possibilities, of Greek tragic metre. For fuller accounts (which, however, require some knowledge of Greek) see:

Oxford Classical Dictionary, article on *metre, Greek*, London: Oxford University Press, 1949.

D. S. Raven, *Greek Metre, an Introduction*, New York: Humanities Press, Inc., 1962.

W. J. W. Koster, *Traité de métrique grecque*, 2nd ed., Leiden: Brill, 1953.

ADAM PARRY

INTRODUCTION

From long before the time of Homer, certain categories of crime were punished by the terrifying powers of the underworld—the Erinyes. Although they primarily avenged crimes committed by offspring against parents, even if such crimes fell short of parricide or matricide, they also punished people who had failed to keep their oaths, as they did in Hesiod.

The Erinyes were probably personified curses; Aeschylus has them say that they are called Curses below the earth (*Eum.* 417). From early times, they seem to have been regarded as the defenders of the natural order of things. Before the word *Dike* came to mean "Justice," it meant "the proper order of nature" or "custom." Early in the fifth century b.c., the Ephesian philosopher Heraclitus said that if the sun exceeded the measure appointed it, the Erinyes, the assistants of Dike, would check it; thus he saw them as the maintainers of the proper order of the universe.

In *The Iliad* (19. 407f) Hera allows Xanthus, the immortal horse of Achilles, to warn his master of approaching death; it is the Erinyes who stop him from speaking. In Hesiod the Erinyes are daughters of Earth, whereas in Aeschylus they are daughters of Night; in either case they belong to the ancient gods, who were mighty long before the birth of Zeus, the present ruler of the universe. Although the cult of the Erinyes was never widely diffused, they were worshiped at several places, particularly in Athens. Despite their terrifying aspect as the punishers of crime, they resembled other underworld divinities in having the power to bestow fertility, and hence prosperity and happiness. Worshipers often referred to them euphemistically as "The Venerable Ones" (Semnai) or "The Kindly Ones" (Eumenides). When Aeschylus has them accept Athene's offer of a home in Athens, he is taking advantage of a long-existing cult and a long-recognized aspect of their character.

Throughout the *Oresteia*, the Erinyes exert a powerful influence on the fortunes of the house of Atreus. They punish Troy for Paris's offense against the laws of hospitality (*Agam.* 59, 749); later Cassandra sees them besieging the house of the Atreidae (*Agam.* 1117, 1190f); and it is to them, together with Dike and Ate, that Clytemnestra claims to have sacrificed her husband. In *The Libation Bearers* we are reminded three times that Agamemnon's murderers must pay the penalty to the Erinyes (402, 651, 577), and we are told that if Orestes should fail to avenge his father, it is they who would inevitably punish him (269f). Yet they will also punish him for the murder of his mother, and in the last scene, visible only to the eyes of Orestes, they appear to hound him from his home. Unlike Agamemnon, Clytemnestra and Aegisthus have no human heirs left to avenge them. Thus in the third play the Erinyes, hitherto seen only by Orestes, must themselves appear to carry out their duty, and they themselves form the Chorus of the play. As in *The Suppliants*, where the daughters of Danaus, the main actors in the story, form the Chorus, here too the Chorus is more than usually involved in the events depicted.

Orestes is confronted with a problem to which there is no satisfactory answer; he should neither kill his mother nor fail to avenge his father. He turns to an institution that at least since the end of the eighth century B.C. exercised a powerful influence on Greek religion and politics—to Apollo's oracle at Delphi. The story that Orestes spent his exile, not as *The Odyssey* claims in Athens, but in Phocis, near Delphi, occurs first in the post-Homeric epic called *Nostoi*, "The Return of the Heroes from Troy" (see note on 841 of *The Libation Bearers*). Stesichorus in the sixth century B.C., a century after *Nostoi*, used it in his *Oresteia*, and also has Apollo

2

protect Orestes against the Erinyes by giving the boy a bow with which to keep them off. During Aeschylus' lifetime, when the oracle gave comfort to the Persian invaders, the influence of the oracle suffered a blow from which it never quite recovered, but even after this, it continued to be very great. Delphi was the acknowledged arbiter on questions of sacral law, religious ritual, and the ceremonies of purification by which the Greeks sought to remove the "pollution" attached to those guilty of certain crimes, especially murder of kindred. According to the usual story, deliberately altered by Aeschylus to save Apollo from the reproach of having used violence (see note on 5), the oracle had first belonged to the primeval earth-goddess. She had been a central figure of Greek religion before the Olympians, and Apollo had conquered the oracle by slaying her sacred snake, the Python. Afterwards, he had undergone a ceremony of purification; and in many cities, including Athens, it was customary for those guilty of involuntary homicide to undergo such a ceremony.

In Aeschylus' play Apollo purifies Orestes by washing him in pig's blood, and after this ceremony, Orestes no longer considers himself polluted. This, however, does not free him from the attentions of the Erinyes, who flatly reject Apollo's order that they should henceforth leave Orestes alone. Strictly speaking, they are within their rights; it is their duty to destroy anyone who has shed his kindred's blood—"his own blood," as the Greeks considered it to be—and to them the plea of extenuating circumstances is irrelevant. Apollo treats Orestes' crime as a case of justifiable homicide and thus grants purification, but the Erinyes bitterly denounce him for having infringed upon their time-honored prerogative. As in *Prometheus*, there is a clash between gods who belong to different generations—the Erinyes, who as daughters of Night are counted among the ancient gods, and Apollo, who is the son of Zeus. This conflict ends, not in the defeat of the representatives of the old order, but in a settlement in which their claims are fully recognized; far from abandoning their ancient functions, they are exalted and dignified with new honors. The play that has begun by horrifying its audience with the gruesome appearance and bloodthirsty threats of the Erinyes ends by honoring them with solemn panegyrics, claiming that they are among the greatest benefactors of mankind.

3

After Orestes, at Apollo's order, has fled from Delphi to Athens, both sides are persuaded by Athene, the patron goddess of Athens, to let her handle the conflict. She chooses to refer it to a group of leading Athenian citizens composing a tribunal over which she herself presides on this occasion. The tribunal takes its seat upon the Hill of Ares, or Areopagus, where in fact the famous Court of Areopagus held its sessions, a court destined to last for centuries and to be the audience for St. Paul's famous sermon (Acts 17:22–31). (For further discussion of the allusions to the Court of the Areopagus and to the Argive alliance, the reader is referred to the Appendix.) The Erinyes are the prosecutors, and Apollo is the advocate of Orestes. Before the votes are cast, Athene announces that if they prove equal she will cast her deciding vote in favor of acquittal, and it is by this vote that Orestes is acquitted.

Some critics have found Athene's reason for voting for Orestes insufferably frivolous, and others have tried to invest it with a wholly imaginary profundity. She says that she had no mother, having sprung fully armed from the head of Zeus, and therefore cannot sympathize with a mother's point of view. In fact Athene, who is the sister of Apollo and the daughter of Zeus, from whom the authority of Apollo's oracles is derived, is likely to sympathize with the plea of extenuating circumstances against the Erinyes' irrational insistence on the letter of the law. But to say so would run the risk of the Erinyes' immediately carrying out their threat to take vengeance on Athens if they lose their case. Instead Athene must regard the situation as a stalemate that can be resolved only by her personal decision; the motive of this decision is less likely to be offensive to the Erinyes if it is personal to the presiding judge.

Orestes takes his leave, with thanks to Athene and promises to her city; his case is settled. It remains for Athene, however, to restrain the Erinyes from carrying out their fearsome threats of destruction against Athens. By a judicious mixture of threats and promises, conveyed with all possible dignity and tact, Athene succeeds in this difficult task. If she wished, she could deal with the Erinyes by force; the younger generation of gods now rules the universe, and she could borrow Zeus's thunder and treat her adversaries as the Titans and the Giants had been treated. But she has no need to do so; by offering them the consolation of a special

4

cult in Athens, she can not only appease their wrath but also win for her city the many blessings that they have the power to give. Nowhere is there any hint that from this time forth the Erinyes are to renounce their cherished functions; on the contrary, Athens' homicide law in Aeschylus' time acknowledged their importance. If the play reflects the transition from the blood-feud to the rule of law, it reflects a transition to a law that explicitly recognized the duty of obtaining redress.

At the beginning of the play, the Erinyes appear as figures of unspeakable horror. When the door of the temple opens to reveal the terrifying beings who, so far unseen, have dominated the action of the two previous plays, the dignified priestess of Apollo, the Pythia, is reduced to panic by their hideous aspect. When the ghost of Clytemnestra rises to wake the sleeping Erinyes with a clamor for revenge, their utterance proves no less frightful than their looks. Apollo denounces them as figures of outmoded horror; they have no place in Hellas, he declares, but in eastern countries, whose barbarous peoples practice torture and mutilation. Yet, at the end of the play these same monstrous and uncanny beings are honored by Apollo's own sister, the tutelary goddess of Athens.

The turning point is the Second Stasimon (490f), the song in which the Erinyes first offer a rational statement of the nature of their office and the reasons for its existence. Were they to cease punishing the killers of kindred, the social order would dissolve. They are the protectors of Dike, goddess of Justice, dear to Zeus; through them Zeus gives to men the "grace that comes by violence" (*Agam.* 182). Far from being primitive relics of a vanished order, as Apollo has maintained, they are pillars of every government, including that of Apollo's own father, Zeus. In the great charge that she delivers to the Areopagus just before the votes are cast (681f), Athene unmistakably echoes the words of the Erinyes in the Second Stasimon. She speaks not of the Erinyes' function in the government of the universe, but of the function of the Areopagus in the government of Athens; her deliberate echoing of their words, therefore, clearly indicates an analogy between the two. By her whole conduct toward the Erinyes, both before and during the trial and during the great conciliation scene following the announcement of the verdict, Athene shows that she recognizes the value and im-

5

portance of their task. The trilogy ends with their triumph, and by the light of flaming torches they are escorted to the shrine where from now on they are to be worshiped with special reverence.

We can thus see how the moral and theological principles implicit in the history of the house of Atreus are connected with the political doctrines shown in the last play of the trilogy. We have witnessed the stern reciprocal justice of Zeus: he who, like Paris or Atreus, commits an outrage against another shall himself (or his descendants) suffer outrage in return. The doer shall suffer and thereby learn the folly of breaking Zeus's law. Profiting from his example, men shall receive the "grace that comes by violence." The Erinyes, serving Zeus's purpose, are there to teach men this legend.

The dreadful action of Atreus sets in motion a chain of successive crimes. In strict logic, there is no reason why it should end before the family has been annihilated. Yet when Orestes, faced with a choice between intolerable decisions, consults Apollo, the god supports him against the Erinyes. Apollo and the Erinyes refer their dispute to the arbitration of a third party, and an issue that admits of no real resolution is arbitrarily resolved by a personal decision. Although the Erinyes lose their victim, they are not defeated or disgraced; on the contrary, they are appeased by the grant of new honors, and the importance of their functions is emphasized. In the city, as in the universe, anarchy and despotism must both equally be avoided; freedom can survive only if it is balanced by the existence of a force that can punish crime. From the history of the house of Atreus, men may learn wisdom. Likewise, the citizens of Athens must learn wisdom in the course of time (1000); they must never expel from their city the force capable of inspiring terror and in whose absence freedom might degenerate into anarchy.

CHARACTERS

APOLLO, son of Zeus

ATHENE, patron goddess of Athens

CHORUS, the Erinyes

THE GHOST OF CLYTEMNESTRA, slain mother of ORESTES

ESCORT, torch-bearers

ORESTES, son of Agamemnon

PYTHIA, priestess of Apollo

THE EUMENIDES

Enter PYTHIA.

PYTHIA   First among the gods in this prayer I honor
the first prophet, Earth; and after her Themis,
she who was the second to take her seat
in this place of prophecy, as a tradition tells; and third

1f PYTHIA: Pronounce *Pié-thi-a*.
    The opening scene takes place in what was, together with the
sanctuary of Zeus at Olympia, the greatest of Greek shrines—
the temple of APOLLO at Delphi. Before APOLLO came to
Greece, the Delphic oracle had belonged to the great earth-
goddess who played an important part in the Minoan and
Mycenaean religions. This fact is clearly reflected in the tradi-
tions of the Greeks about the oracle's early history. Our
earliest account of the oracle's beginnings is contained in the
Homeric "Hymn to Apollo," a work hardly later than the
seventh century B.C. Indeed the hymn does not allude to an
oracle before APOLLO's time; but it tells how, in order to
win the site for his own, APOLLO had to fight and kill the
great serpent, the Python. Euripides, in a choral ode in his
play *Iphigeneia in Tauris* (1249f), says that before the oracle

9

belonged to APOLLO it was owned by Themis, goddess of righteousness. Themis, the mother of the Titan Prometheus according to one story, belonged to the earlier generation of gods, before the time of Zeus and his son APOLLO. She was often identified with Ge or Gaia, the earth-goddess. According to Euripides, and this was undoubtedy the oldest story, APOLLO forcibly dispossessed her. The snake in Greek religion is often associated with subterranean powers, and the Python must have been the sacred guardian snake of the earth-goddess; indeed, in the oldest version of the legend he may have been identical with her. The belief that Delphi was the center of the earth probably goes back to the oracle's earliest period. The ancient stone known as the omphalos (navel), supposedly marking the earth's center, may date from this time. The earth was supposed to send up messages from below (see *The Libation Bearers.* 807f with note).

In Hesiod's poem, *Theogony,* which gave an authoritative account of the genealogy of the gods, Gaia (Earth) was the consort of Ouranos (Heaven), the first ruler of the universe. Themis was their daughter and the sister of their son Kronos, who succeeded Ouranos upon his throne and was finally ousted by his son Zeus. Clearly Gaia's time as the possessor of the oracle was meant to coincide with the reign of Ouranos and Themis' time, to coincide with the reign of Kronos; when Zeus overthrew Kronos, APOLLO, Zeus's son, could replace Themis as the god of Delphi. Aeschylus, however, was eager to avoid the story that APOLLO violently dispossessed his venerable relative. This is why Aeschylus makes Themis voluntarily hand over the oracle to her sister Phoebe. Phoebe was the mother of APOLLO's mother Leto, and APOLLO's name, "Phoebus," is the masculine form of her name. It was therefore easy for Aeschylus to have APOLLO acquire the oracle as a birthday present from his own grandmother.

Aeschylus liked to begin a play with a momentous word or phrase, often a divine name occurring in a prayer. Thus *The Suppliants* begins with "Zeus" and *Agamemnon* with "To the gods I pray"; *The Libation Bearers* begins with the prayer of Orestes to Hermes; and a lost play, probably the first of

in succession, with the consent of Themis, and with no vio-
lence done to any,   5
another Titaness, a child of Earth, took her seat here,
Phoebe. And she gave it as a birthday gift
to Phoebus; and he bears a name taken from hers.
Leaving the lake and ridge of Delos,
sailing to the ship-frequented coasts of Pallas,   10
he came to this land and to his seat upon Parnassus.
He was escorted on his way with solemn reverence
by sons of Hephaestus, the road-makers who made tame
the land before untamed.
And when he came he had great honor from the people,   15

Aeschylus' trilogy about Achilles and the death of Hector, begins "To Zeus's majesty I first do reverence" (frag. 283 in the Loeb edition, vol. ii).

5   *Themis:* pronounce *Themm-is.*

Stress is laid on the voluntary nature of the transfer because the story that APOLLO took the oracle by force was so well known.

9   *Delos:* pronounce *Deé-los.*

APOLLO's other famous shrine at Delos, his birthplace, was older than the one at Delphi. Excavation, however, has now confirmed that his mother Leto and his sister Artemis (originally identical with the earth-goddess and her daughter) were established on Delos before he was. The lake and Mount Cynthus are the two most conspicuous features of the holy island.

10 The coasts of Pallas are the coasts of Athens, Pallas being another name of ATHENE, the patron goddess of Athens.

11 Delphi stands on a slope of Mount Parnassus; above it tower the twin peaks of the great mountain, the Phaedriades, and below it the cliffs drop sheer to the gorge of the river Pleistos.

12f *Hephaestus:* pronounce *He-feé-stus.*

The Athenians are called "children of Hephaestus" because of the story that their legendary ancestor, Erichthonius, was the son of Hephaestus and the earth-goddess.

11

and from Delphus, the king seated at the tiller of the land.
And Zeus made his mind inspired with the diviner's art
and set him up as the fourth prophet on this throne:
Loxias is the spokesman of his father Zeus.
These are the gods I place in the forefront of my prayer;   20
and in my speech I honor Pallas who dwells before the
      temple;
and I revere the nymphs, who live in the Corycian cave,
hollow, dear to birds, the haunt of gods.
And Bromios has dwelt in the region, nor do I forget him,

---

16   The Delphians traced their descent from a mythical Delphus,
supposed to be descended from the earth-goddess and her consort.

19   The word translated "spokesman" is *prophetes,* the Greek
word from which "prophet" is derived. Originally it simply
meant "spokesman"; the notion that the prefix *pro-* meant
"before" and that *prophetes* meant "one who foretells the
future" arose only later. "Loxias" is the name of APOLLO in
his capacity as an oracular god, and it supposedly derived from
the deviousness of his oracles (*loxos* means "crooked").

21   The shrine of Athene Pronaia (before the temple) lies a
good way east of the temple of APOLLO, near the cleft of
Castalia. Very likely this was the original site of the cult; ex-
cavations have shown that worship continued there from
prehellenic times, long before the foundation of the classical
sanctuary of APOLLO.

22   *Corycian:* pronounce *Kore-iss-ian.* The Corycian cave, which has
the same name as another famous cave at Corycus in Cilicia, is
high up near the summit of Parnassus (about 8,200 feet high);
the visit takes two days and a night. Like other mountain caves,
it was thought to be a haunt of Pan and the nymphs.

24–   From at least as early as the seventh century B.C., Dionysus
26   —Bromios is one of his names—had been accepted at
Delphi. The brothers were even said to share the place,
Dionysus being at home there in the winter months, while

ever since the host of Bacchants had the god for leader, 25
and he contrived for Pentheus the death of a hunted hare.
On the waters of Pleistos and on Poseidon's might
do I call, and on Zeus the Fulfiller, the Most High;
and so I take my seat as prophetess.
And now may they grant me far better fortune than in my
  goings in 30

APOLLO was away in the land of his favorite people, the Hyperboreans, in the remote north. Festivals held every two years at Delphi, at which women danced during the night to the light of torches in honor of Dionysus, are mentioned by the poets (e.g., Sophocles, *Antigone* 1126f) and continued well into historical times. In this passage, Aeschylus dates Dionysus' establishment at Delphi from the time of the god's legendary conquest of Greece. In a lost play called the *Xantriai* Aeschylus told, or at least mentioned, the story of how Dionysus punished his cousin Pentheus (pronounce *Penth'-yuse*), king of Thebes, for denying his divinity. Dionysus inspired Pentheus' mother and aunts with frenzy, making them tear Pentheus to pieces; the story is handled by Euripides in his extant play *The Bacchants.*

27 *Pleistos*: pronounce *Plicé-tos; Poseidon*: pronounce *Pos-eyé-don.*
For a comment on the Pleistos, the river of Delphi, see note on 11 above. In classical religion Poseidon figures as brother of Zeus and lord of the sea, but he had originally been the consort of the Minoan-Mycenaean earth-goddess. He had therefore been honored at Delphi from an early time; in historic times he had an altar inside APOLLO's temple. There was a story that he originally owned Delphi but exchanged it with APOLLO for another shrine.

28 "The Fulfiller" and "the Most High" were both cult-titles of Zeus; for the former compare *Agam.* 973 and *The Suppliants* 525; and for the latter *Agam.* 55, 509.

30 In primitive prayers the worshiper regularly asked the god to grant him favor greater than he ever had before.

13

THE EUMENIDES

in time past; and if any of the Greeks are present,
let them enter in order of the lot, as is the custom;
for I prophesy as the god may lead me.

> She opens the door of the temple and goes in,
> but comes out almost immediately.

Dread to tell of and dread for the eyes to see
is the thing that has sent me back from the house of Loxias,   35
so that I have no strength left and cannot hold myself up-
    right,
I run with the aid of my hands, not with swift feet;
for an old woman afraid is nothing, no better than a child.
I was on my way to the inner chamber with its many chaplets,
and I saw upon the navel-stone a man polluted in the sight of
    the gods,   40
seated there as a suppliant;

---

31 The oracle was originally for the Greeks, and they were supposed to have precedence over foreigners. Originally the order of consultation was determined by lot, as here, though later the Delphians awarded special precedence to particular states and individuals.

37 The ancient commentary on the play interprets this as meaning that PYTHIA is on all fours. But it may mean that her hands are trembling.

39 The inner shrine, like the omphalos or "navel-stone" (40), was hung with garlands to mark its sacred character.

41 The blood is presumably the pig's blood used by APOLLO to purify ORESTES from the pollution caused by murder (see 280–83 below). Purification from blood-guilt was an important idea in Delphic religion as early as the seventh century B.C. In this play ORESTES is regarded as being freed by his purification from the provisions of the interdict against speaking to a polluted person, allowing him to enter one's house, or taking part in worship (see 443f); but it does not cause the Erinyes (pronounce I'-rin-ē-ez) to give up their pursuit.

his hands and newly drawn sword were dripping with blood,
and he held a branch of olive grown on high,
a branch wreathed in reverent fashion with a great tuft of
    wool,
a silvery fleece (for so I shall describe it clearly).   45
And in front of this man slept a wondrous troop
of women, seated upon chairs.
Not women, but Gorgons I call them;
no, not even to the shape of Gorgons can I compare them.
I have seen before now paintings of those that carried off   50
the feast of Phineus; but these appear wingless,
black, altogether hateful in their ways;
and they snore with a blast unapproachable,
and from their eyes they drip a loathsome liquid.
And their attire is such as one should not bring   55
near to the statues of the gods nor into the houses of men.
I have not seen the tribe this company belongs to,
nor the land that can boast to breed this race
unscathed, and not repent of its labor.
The outcome now must be the care of the master   60
of this house, the mighty Loxias himself.
He is both healer-seer and prophet,
and can purify the halls of others.

    Exit PYTHIA; the central door now opens reveal-

---

43   An olive branch was customarily carried by suppliants. Such
    branches had chaplets made of wool hanging upon them (e.g.,
    Iliad 1. 14f).

48   The obvious point of resemblance to Gorgons was their hav-
    ing snakes for hair.

51   *Phineus*: pronounce *Fine'-yuse*. Phineus was persecuted by the
    bird-women known as Harpies, who flew down and seized his
    food before he could eat it.

54   Their eyes dripped blood (cf. *The Libation Bearers* 1058).

55– They wore long black robes (cf. *The Libation Bearers* 1049);
56   these seem to have been dirty and ragged.

ing APOLLO and ORESTES inside the temple; the
sleeping Erinyes recline on chairs.

APOLLO   *I will not abandon you; but I will guard you to*
  the end,
whether by your side or far removed,   65
and I will not grow gentle to your enemies.
And now you see these mad ones overcome;
the despicable creatures have fallen in sleep, gray
virgins, ancient maidens, with whom no god
nor any among men nor any beast has intercourse.   70
For the sake of evil they came into being, since evil
darkness and Tartarus below the earth is their portion,
loathed as they are by men and by Olympian gods.
Nonetheless fly from them, and do not grow faint!
For they will drive you over all the wide mainland,   75
striding ever over the earth you tread in your wanderings,
and beyond the sea and seagirt cities.
Do not grow weary as you struggle to cope with this
ordeal; but go to the city of Pallas
and sit there, taking her ancient image in your arms.   80
And there shall we have judges of your cause, and words
to charm them, and shall discover means
to release you forever from this distress;
for it was I who persuaded you to slay your mother.

ORESTES   Lord Apollo, you know how to be righteous;   85

---

64 APOLLO's language recalls the formulas used in prayers ad-
    dressed to the gods for such protection.
67 The manner of the transition suggests that the sleep of the
    Erinyes is due to a charm cast upon them by APOLLO, who
    would have wanted no disturbance during the rite of purifica-
    tion he had just performed.
72 *Tartarus*: pronounce *Tart'-ar-us*.
79 Athens, where there was an ancient wooden image of ATHENE.
85f Athenian law distinguished between criminal offenses and

16

but since you have that skill, learn also not to be neglectful
But your strength renders sure your power for good.

APOLLO   Remember, let not fear overcome your mind.
And you, my brother, son of the same father,
Hermes, guard him; true altogether to your title,   90
be his escort, as you protect this my suppliant.
Zeus, I say, respects this sanctity of outlaws
that is sent to men with auspicious guidance.

> Exeunt APOLLO and ORESTES; CLYTEMNESTRA'S
> GHOST appears.

CLYTEMNESTRA   Sleep on! Aha! And what is the use of you
    asleep?
And I, thus dishonored at your hands   95
among the other dead—the reproach
of the deeds of blood I did still lives on among the departed,
as in indignity I wander; I declare to you

---

86   offenses due to negligence, and the wording here suggests that
the poet has this distinction in mind.

89   APOLLO's address to Hermes does not prove that Hermes is
present on the stage; a god may be addressed whether he is
present or not.

91   The words allude to a well-known cult-title of Hermes, "The
Escorter."

92   "Outlaws" here means "suppliants," who were traditionally
under the special protection of Zeus.

94   The GHOST's indignation that the Erinyes can sleep at such a
time and its injunction to them to take action that will
remedy its own plight in Hades recall the words of the ghost
of Patroclus to the sleeping Achilles in The Iliad (23. 69f);
but CLYTEMNESTRA's indignation is more bitter, as suits her
character and the circumstances.

17

that they level a most grievous charge at me
who suffered so sorely at the hands of my nearest kin—   100
none among the divinities is angry on my account,
slaughtered as I was by matricidal hands.
See these wounds in your heart!   103
Full many an offering of mine have you lapped up;   106
libations without wine, sober appeasements,
and solemn feasts by night upon the hearth that housed the
    fire
I burned, at an hour not shared by any of the gods.
And all this I see trampled under foot;   110
and he is gone, he has escaped you swiftly as a fawn;
he has leapt easily, from the middle of your net,
mightily mocking you.
Listen, for on my plea depends
my whole existence. Take heed, goddesses below the earth,   115
for as a shadow I, Clytemnestra, now invoke you!

The Erinyes in their sleep utter whining sounds.

---

103   This line is followed in the manuscripts by two lines that
    mean:

    For in sleep your mind has eyes that shine brightly;
    but by day the fate of mortals cannot be foreseen
    [or, possibly, "mortals can see ahead"].

    The first of these lines could make sense in the context; the
    second, whichever of several different possible interpretations
    is adopted, seems to make none, and it is probably interpolated.
    Although the first line might be genuine, I am inclined to
    think that it came from the same context as the second and
    that both were jotted down in the margin by some reader as a
    parallel passage, then included in the text by mistake.

107   Wine was never offered to the Erinyes, who preferred water
    and honey. Like other gods who lived below the earth, they
    received sacrifices at night.

109   gods: probably used in the sense of "Olympian gods," as at
    Agam. 637.

18

CLYTEMNESTRA *Whine if you will, but the man is gone
far off in flight;*
for suppliants are not without friends.

Again the whining sound.   120

CLYTEMNESTRA *You are all too drowsy; you have no pity
for my suffering;*
and Orestes, killer of me, his mother, is gone.

The Erinyes make a moaning sound.

CLYTEMNESTRA *You moan, you are drowsy; up, up, quick,
get up!*
What task has fate assigned to you but to wreak trouble?   125

Again the moaning.

CLYTEMNESTRA *Sleep and weariness, powerful conspirators,*
have reduced to nothing the dread serpent's power.

The Erinyes twice make a shrill, whining sound.

CHORUS *Seize him! Seize him! Seize him! Seize him! Mark!* 130

CLYTEMNESTRA *In a dream you pursue your beast, and you
bay like*
a hound that never ceases to think of the chase!
What are you at? Up, do not be overcome by weariness!
Do not be ignorant of my pain, made soft by sleep!
Let my just reproaches sting your heart!   135
For to the righteous these are goads.
Waft your bloody breath upon him!
Dry him up with its vapor, your womb's fire!
After him, shrivel him up in a renewed pursuit!

---

129 *serpent:* the Erinyes who were often portrayed in snake form.
137 The Erinyes are repeatedly said to shrivel their victims by
sucking up all their blood; they themselves drip blood from
their eyes as well as breathing it out.

19

CHORUS Wake up and then wake your neighbor as I wake
 you!   140
Do you sleep? Up, cast away sleep,
and let us see if in this prelude there is any fault!

STROPHE 1

Ho, ho! Out upon it! We have suffered, dear ones—
much have I suffered, and all in vain!—
we have suffered a grievous blow, alas,   145
a hurt unbearable.
Slipped from the net and vanished is the beast:
Vanquished by sleep, I have lost my prey.

ANTISTROPHE 1

Ah, son of Zeus! You are a thief!
Young as you are, you have ridden us down, aged divinities— 150

---

142 prelude: refers to the ghost dream that the Erinyes have just
   had.

143 The meter of the parodos is dochmiac (◡ –– ◡ –) mixed
   with iambic; the dochmiacs, as usual expressive of violent
   emotion (see The Libation Bearers, 152f), easily prevail. The
   second strophe (155–61) and its antistrophe (162–68) are
   marked by an especially close symmetry; 159 and its antistrophic
   line, 165, each consist of a preposition governing a noun and
   then the same preposition governing a second noun:

    hypo phrenas, hypo lobon peri poda, peri kara
   Each is followed by a sentence beginning with the same main
   verb paresti, here rendered "it is mine."

144 This line (like its antistrophic line 150, and also 147 ~ 154,
   155 ~ 162, 169 ~ 174) is an iambic trimeter, just like the
   iambic trimeters that are the usual meter of dialogue. But like
   the rest of the ode, these trimeters will be sung and not spoken.

150 The motif of a conflict between older and younger genera-

respecting the suppliant, a godless man,
hateful to parents.
You have stolen away the matricide, god that you are!
What is there in this that any shall say is just?

STROPHE 2

To me in my dreams there came reproach, 155
and smote me like a charioteer
with goad grasped in the middle,
under my heart, under my vitals.
It is mine to feel cruel, most cruel, 160
the sting of the public scourger's cruel lash!

ANTISTROPHE 2

Such are the actions of the younger gods,
whose might goes altogether beyond justice.
The throne drips blood,
about its foot, about its head! 165
It is ours to see earth's navel-stone stained
with a grim pollution it has got from deeds of blood.

STROPHE 3

With defilement at the hearth, seer that he is,
he has stained his own sanctuary by his own impulse, his own
  summons, 170

---

tions of the gods is important in this play, as it is in *Prometheus*. In *Prometheus* the hero, as a Titan and a son of Earth, belongs to a generation older than that of his enemy Zeus. In *The Eumenides* the Erinyes, as daughters of Night, also belong to the older generation of gods (cf. 162f).

honoring things mortal beyond what the gods' law permits,
and destroying the ancient dispensations of the fates.

ANTISTROPHE 3

To me too he is hateful, and that man shall be never free;
though he flee beneath the earth, he shall never gain his
*   liberty.*   175
He shall come stained with the guilt of murder
to where he shall get upon his head another to pollute him.

    Enter APOLLO.

    APOLLO   Out of this house with all speed, I command you!
Be off, leave my prophetic chambers,   180
for fear you get a winged, glistening snake,
sped from my bowstring wrought of gold,
and disgorge in agony a dark froth from humans,
as you vomit up clots of the blood that you have sucked!
It is not fitting you should come to this house;   185
your place is where sentence is given to lop off heads and
    gouge out eyes,
where murders are, and by destruction of the seed

---

172   The Erinyes mean that APOLLO is preventing them from
fulfilling the functions allotted to them by an ancient dispensation.

176– *He*: ORESTES who is himself a cause of pollution. When the
177 Erinyes threaten that he will get another to pollute him, they
mean that he will become a victim of the Alastor, the personified family curse, to which this description can also be
applied. The Erinyes are often said to leap upon the heads of
their victims.

186 APOLLO means that the Erinyes do not belong in Greece but
in some country inhabited by barbarians. All the practices referred to in this passage were in vogue among the Persians
and could be illustrated from the account given of them by
Herodotus.

the manhood of the young is ruined, and there are mutilations
and stoning, and men moan in long lament,
impaled beneath the spine. Do you not hear   190
what sort of feast it is that you so love
that the gods detest you? The whole fashion of your form
suggests it. The den of a blood-lapping lion
should be the habitation of such creatures; you should not in
    this place
of oracle rub off contagion on those near you.   195
Be off, a flock without a shepherd!
Such a herd is loved by none among the gods.

CHORUS   Lord Apollo, hear in turn our answer!
You yourself are no mere abettor of this deed;
but in all things you have so acted that the blame is yours
    alone.   200

APOLLO   How so? Extend your speech just far enough to
tell me.

CHORUS   Your oracle told the stranger to kill his mother.

APOLLO   Yes, it did, thereby ordaining vengeance for his
father. Why not?

CHORUS   And then you promised to receive him, with
blood fresh on his hands.

APOLLO   Yes, and I told him to come as suppliant to this
house.   205

CHORUS   And then do you revile us for acting as his escort?

APOLLO   Yes; you are not fit to approach this house.

CHORUS   But this is the task assigned to us. . . .

APOLLO   What privilege do you speak of? Proudly tell of
your noble prerogative!

194– The notion that pollution could be "rubbed off onto" others
195 occurs even in a speech by the late fifth-century orator
     Antiphon.

23

CHORUS We drive from their homes the killers of their
mothers.   210

APOLLO And what of a woman who has slain her
husband?

CHORUS That would not be the
shedding of one's own blood with one's own hand.

APOLLO Indeed you dishonor and reduce to nothing
the pledges of Hera the Fulfiller and of Zeus,
and the Cyprian is cast aside in dishonor by your plea,   215
she from whom comes to mortals what they hold most dear.
For the marriage bed, granted by fate to man and woman,
is mightier than an oath, if Justice is its guardian.
So if you allow to those that kill their partners
such license that you do not requite them nor visit them with
    your wrath,   220
I say that your pursuit of Orestes is not just.
For the one crime I see that you greatly take to heart,
while in the other matter you are manifestly milder.
But the goddess Pallas shall review this case.

CHORUS I shall never leave that man!   225

APOLLO Well, pursue him, and give yourself more trouble.

CHORUS Do not speak as though you would curtail my
privileges!

---

212 Blood relations were thought of as having the same
blood. Thus in Sophocles' *Oedipus the King* Oedipus can
speak of having shed *his own* blood when referring to his killing
of his father (1400).

214 Hera is called "The Fulfiller" (*Teleia*) in her capacity as goddess of marriage; Zeus the Fulfiller was associated with her
in this cult, and their marriage was the archetype of all marriages.

215 *the Cyprian:* a name of Aphrodite.

224 APOLLO has already told ORESTES to go to Athens (79–80).

APOLLO Even if your privileges were offered me, I would
refuse them.

CHORUS Yes, for in any case you are accounted great by
Zeus's throne.
But, since a mother's blood drives me on, with my charge   230
I will pursue this man and hunt him down.

APOLLO And I will protect him and will guard the
suppliant.
For dread among mortals and among the gods
is the wrath of him who has implored mercy, if one willingly
betrays him.

The scene changes to Athens; enter ORESTES.

ORESTES Queen Athene, I have come at Loxias' bidding.   235
Graciously receive a wretched man,
not needing to be purified nor with unclean hands,
but with his guilt's edge already blunted and worn off
against other habitations and traveled ways of men.
Crossing over land and sea alike,   240
and keeping the oracular commands of Loxias,
I come to your house; your image, goddess,
will I guard here as I await the issue of the trial.

Enter the Erinyes.

---

235 Changes of scene do not occur in any tragedy known to us
later than Aeschylus, but in early tragedy they may have been
more easily allowed. Aeschylus' play *The Women of Etna* had
no less than four, as we have learned from a papyrus published in
1952 (see frag. 287 in the Loeb edition). The scene has
changed to the ancient temple of ATHENE on the Acropolis.

237 See note on 41.

242 APOLLO has told ORESTES to clasp the image of the goddess
(80); this image is presumably visible on the stage, for the
Erinyes mention at 259 that ORESTES is holding it.

Chorus *Just so! Here can the man's trail be clearly seen!
Follow the guidance of the voiceless informer!*   245
*Yes, like a hound after a wounded fawn
by the drops of blood do we track him down.
My many labors, deadly to men, leave my breast panting;
for I have ranged through every place on earth
and beyond the sea in wingless flight
I have come pursuing, not slower than a ship.
And now he must be cowering somewhere here;
the scent of human blood, so familiar, greets me!*

*Look, look again!
Scan every spot,*   255
*that the killer of his mother may not escape us in flight,
    unpunished.*

They catch sight of Orestes.

*Here he is. Once more he has protection,
and with arms twined about the image of the immortal goddess
seeks to stand trial for the debt he owes.*   260
*But that may not be. His mother's blood upon the ground
is hard to gather up. Faugh!
Gone, spilt on the ground, is the liquid!
No, in atonement while you still live you must let us swill
the rich, red offering from your limbs; from you*   265
may I win myself a meal—a cruel drink!

---

244 "Epiparodos" means a second entry of the Chorus, a rare oc-
currence in tragedy. The change of scene has required the
Chorus, contrary to custom, to leave the stage (231); they
now return. First, the Coryphaeus speaks in dialogue meter
(244–53); then, the Chorus sings (254–75). The meter is
dochmiac, but iambic trimeters occur sporadically (261, 264,
267, 269, 272–73); it is very like the meter of the Parodos, but
lacks strophic responsion.

261 See note on *The Libation Bearers* 49.

Still living I shall dry you up and hale you down below,
so that in requital you may pay with sorrow for your
    mother's murder.
And if any other mortal who has wronged
a god or a stranger,   270
with impious action, or his dear parents,
you shall see how each has the reward Justice ordains.
For Hades is mighty in holding mortals to account
below the earth,
and with mind that records them in its tablets he surveys
    all things.   275

ORESTES   Schooled by misery, I know well
many ways of purifying, and I know where speech is proper
and where silence; and in this instance
it is a wise teacher who has ordered me to speak.
For the blood upon my hand grows drowsy and fades,   280
and the pollution of my mother's killing can be washed away;
while still fresh at the hearth of the god
it was expelled through Phoebus' cleansing by means of
slaughtered swine.

---

273   Aeschylus in *The Suppliants* 230f speaks of a Zeus below the
earth trying the dead for their crimes. (There and at 158 of the
same play he calls Hades "the second Zeus," echoing Homer,
The Iliad 9. 457.) The metaphor of writing in a book recalls a
passage from an unknown lost play of Aeschylus preserved in a
papyrus (see frag. 282 in the Loeb edition), in which the
goddess of Justice herself describes to the CHORUS how she
enters men's crimes in the book of Zeus.

277– The knowledge of when to speak and when to keep silent may
278 be classed among the means of preserving ritual purity, for
abstention from ill-omened utterance (*euphemia*) formed a
regular part of most religious rituals. In this case it is of
course essential that ATHENE and the inhabitants of Athens
know that ORESTES has been purified by APOLLO.

283 *Phoebus:* pronounce *Fee'-bus.*

It would take long to tell the tale from the beginning,
to how many I have come without my company proving
    baneful;   285
Time purifies all things as it grows old with them.
And now with pure lips I call in pious accents
on this country's queen, Athene,
to come to help me; and without the spear she shall acquire
me and my country and the Argive people   290
as an ally to be trusted truly and forever.
But whether in the region of the Libyan land

284– Since it was probably believed that the presence of an ac-
285 cursed person could bring disaster upon innocent people who
were in his company, ORESTES can offer the absence of such a
disaster as proof of his freedom from pollution. Similarly, the
client for whom Antiphon wrote one of his speeches points to
the safe arrival of a ship on which he has traveled as proof of
his innocence of the charge of murder.

286 This line seems otiose to modern taste, and it may well be
a parallel passage written in the margin by a reader and later
copied by mistake into the text; but it is not quite safe to
assume that this is so since the ancients often allowed such
generalizing comments in places where no modern writer would
insert them.

287 The whole speech so far has been uttered in order to justify
the claim now made.

288 ATHENE: pronounce *Ath-een'-ee*.

289 This is the first of the passages in the play that seem to refer
to the alliance between Athens and Argos existing at the time
of the first production (see Appendix, p. 76).

290 *Argive*: pronounce *Ar-gyve* [hard "g"].

292 In early times those who invoked a god begged him to come
from wherever he happened to be, specifying each of his
favorite haunts to be sure of being heard (see for one example among many the prayer to Apollo at *Iliad* 16. 514f).

    In historical times ATHENE's Homeric epithet of Tritogeneia

about the stream of Triton, river of her birth,
she plants her leg erect or covered,
bringing succor to her friends, or makes the Phlegrean plain,   295
like a bold commander, the object of her survey,
may she come—for she hears me even from afar, goddess that
    she is—
that she may grant me release from this my plight!

    CHORUS Not Apollo, I say, or mighty Athene
shall save you from going all neglected   300
down to ruin, not knowing where in your mind joy can dwell,
a bloodless shadow, food for spirits.
Do you not deign to answer? Do you reject my words,
you who have been fattened up for me and consecrated to me?

---

was connected with Lake Tritonis in Libya, not far from
Cyrene, which was said to be her birthplace. Thus it is not
unnatural for Lake Tritonis to be mentioned as one of the
places where ATHENE may happen to be. Still, the poet may
have in mind the presence in Egypt, at the time of the production of this play, of an Athenian force despatched to help
a local prince, Inaros, in his revolt against the Persians.

293   *Triton:* pronounce *Try'-ton; Phlegrean:* pronounce *fleg-ree'-an.*
294   This is simply a highly metaphorical way of saying "is walking
or sitting"; either the leg (Greek says "foot") is erect or it is
covered, as she sits, by her robes.

295   The Phlegrean plain, on Pallene (now Kassandra), one of the
three prongs of Chalcidice, in Macedonia, was the traditional
site of the Battle of the Gods and Giants, in which ATHENE
took a leading part. Those who are eager to find an allusion
to the Athenian expedition to Egypt in the passage immediately
preceding this have suggested that there may have been fighting in this region at the time of the first production; but there
is no independent evidence for this.

304   The Erinyes compare ORESTES to a sacrificial beast, which is
especially fattened for sacrifice to a god. In his case, however,
no sacrifice at an altar is intended; the Erinyes plan to suck
his blood while he is still alive.

I shall feast on you alive, not after sacrifice by an altar;   305
and you shall hear this song to bind you fast!

Come and let us join hands in the dance,
for it is our purpose
to display our grim minstrelsy,
and to tell how our company discharges   310
its office among men!
We claim to walk straight in the path of justice.

---

306   Spells intended to bind the victim have survived in large numbers and are usually inscribed on leaden tablets. They contain such formulas as "I bind and have bound your hands and feet and tongue and soul" or (in a charm designed to influence the result of a race) "Bind the horses' legs and check their power to start and leap and run." Most of the examples date from as late as the Roman Empire, but they are mentioned by Plato and must have existed long before his time.

307   Like a number of Aeschylean parodoi and stasima, the Binding Song is preceded by a prelude in marching anapaests. In this prelude the Erinyes insist on the essential justness of the manner in which they carry out their duties. This theme is elaborated not only in the ode that follows (321f) but even more explicitly in the Second Stasimon (490f).

312ff The connection of the Erinyes with Justice is stressed in the Second Stasimon (see especially 511–25).

    The meter of the first strophe and antistrophe (321–27 and 333–40), like that of the ephymnium that follows each of them (328–34 and 341–46), is mostly trochaic; frequent resolutions cause a slow and solemn effect. Then with the second strophe and antistrophe (349–59 and 360–66), the Erinyes change to a wholly different meter, long dactylic lines, the first period being rounded off by the pherecratean (xx –⌣⌣– x: 351–62) and the second by a kind of trochaic verse that occurs frequently in the first part of the ode. The second strophe is followed by another trochaic stanza; it is possible, though not certain, that it should be inserted after the second antistrophe

Upon him whose hands are clean in act
comes no wrath from us;
he lives out his life unscathed.   315
But if any man, like this one, transgresses
and tries to hide his bloody hands,
as truthful witnesses by the dead
we stand, and as avengers of blood
to him with full power are we made manifest.   320

STROPHE 1

Mother who bore me,
mother Night, to be a punishment for those in darkness
and for those who see the light
hear me! For Leto's son
is trying to rob me of my honor
by taking from me this   325
cowering hare, one rightly consecrated
to the appeasement of his mother's blood.

---

also (after 356), as is done in the Oxford text. The third strophic pair resembles the second; again dactyls are rounded off by a trochaic line (371 ~ 80), and again the strophe, and perhaps the antistrophe also, is followed by a trochaic stanza (372–76), as in the Oxford text. The fourth strophe and antistrophe are prevailingly iambic. The iambic meter (x – ⌣ –) has an obvious affinity with the trochaic (_ ⌣ _ x, and the transition is an easy one. These iambics have an effect of special solemnity, heightened by the substitution in two places (at the end of 383 ~ 391 and 387 ~ 394) of a spondee (– –) for the regular iambic metron (x – ⌣ –).

321 In the *Theogony* of Hesiod, Night was a daughter of the primeval Chaos; she thus suggests immemorial antiquity as well as darkness. Hesiod makes her the mother of the Fates, but Earth the mother of the Erinyes. In Aeschylus, as in Sophocles, the Fates as well as the Erinyes are children of Night.

31

REFRAIN 1

Over our victim
we sing this song, maddening the brain,
carrying away the sense, destroying the mind,   330
a hymn that comes from the Erinyes,
fettering the mind, sung
without the lyre, withering to mortals.

ANTISTROPHE 1

For this is the office that Fate
with her piercing stroke has ordained
that I should hold fast: 335
that after mortals to whom has come
wanton murder of their own,
I should follow, until
they descend below the earth; and after death
no wide liberty is theirs.   340

REFRAIN 1

Over our victim
we sing this song, maddening the brain,
carrying away the sense, destroying the mind,
a hymn that comes from the Erinyes,
fettering the mind, sung   345
without the lyre, withering to mortals.

---

328   The word translated as "victim" is a passive participle, im-
      plying that ORESTES has already been sacrificed.

329   The Erinyes traditionally madden their victims; ORESTES goes
      mad when they first appear in the last scene of *The Libation
      Bearers*.

332   The lyre was associated with happy occasions (compare *Agam.*
      990). The Binding Song was no doubt accompanied on the
      aulos, a pipe somewhat like a clarinet.

STROPHE 2

At our birth, I say, the grant of this office was ordained;
but we must keep our hands off the immortals, nor is
    there any   350
that shares the feasts of both alike;
and in white robes I have no lot or share

· · · · · ·

REFRAIN 2

For I have chosen the ruin
of households; when violence   355
nurtured in the home strikes a dear one down
after it in pursuit we go,
and mighty though the killer be,
we put him in darkness through the fresh blood on his hands.

ANTISTROPHE 2

Eager to exempt some one of the gods from this concern,   360
denying to our prayers fulfillment

---

349 The Erinyes continually stress the antiquity of their powers which have been given them by their sisters, the Fates (cf. 172, 333f, etc.).

350 The worship of the subterranean gods was kept wholly apart from that of the Olympians. Black was the characteristic color of the immortals below the earth.

360– The text is altogether uncertain at this point. If the version
366 I have translated is correct, the sense seems to be that Zeus has decreed that the Erinyes shall have nothing to do with the Olympian gods in order to save one of the Olympians from being pursued by them. The god in question may have been Ares, who according to a well-known story was arraigned before the Areopagus at Athens for the killing of Halirrhothius, son of Poseidon; but we hear nowhere that he was pursued by the Erinyes.

and forbidding us to make inquiry,
Zeus has held our bloodstained, hateful race   365
unworthy of his converse.

STROPHE 3

But the glories of men, for all their splendor beneath the
*   light of day,*
wither away and vanish below the earth, dishonored,
before the onslaught of our black raiment and the dancing   370
of our feet, instinct with malice.

For in truth leaping
from on high, with heavy fall
I bring down my foot;
my legs trip the runner,   375
swift though he be, with an irresistible doom.

ANTISTROPHE 3

And as he falls he knows it not, by reason of the blight that
*   drives him mad;*
such is the darkness of pollution that hovers over a man;
and a murky mist spreads over his house, as is proclaimed
by rumor, bringing many a sigh.   380

STROPHE 4

For the ordinance abides; skilled in contrivance
and strong to accomplish evil

---

370   Like other odes sung by tragic choruses, this was accompanied
      by dances executed by the CHORUS. The mention of leaping
      probably gives some notion of what kind of dance accom-
      panied the words at this point.

and mindful of it are we, awesome
and inexorable to men;
unhonored and unesteemed is the office   385
we pursue, apart from the gods
in the sunless slime;
it makes rough the path of the seeing
and of the blind alike.

ANTISTROPHE 4

Who then among mortals
feels not awe and dread,   390
hearing from me the covenant
ordained by fate and granted by the gods
so that it is valid? Still for me
remains my ancient privilege, nor
do I lack honor,
though it is beneath the ground that I have my station,   395
inhabiting the sunless gloom.

Enter ATHENE.

ATHENE   From far off I heard the sound of your summons,
from the Scamander, while I was taking possession of the land

---

383   The word translated "awesome" is *semnai*, sometimes used as
a euphemism for the Erinyes, "the dread ones," themselves.
Here its effect is enhanced by substituting its two long syllables
for the iambic metron $(x - \smile -)$.

387   Slime is a regular feature of ancient descriptions of the underworld.

388   *the seeing . . . blind:* "the living and the dead"; the latter
live in the darkness of the underworld (cf. 322).

391   The word translated by "covenant" is the solemn word
thesmos, which responds metrically with *semnai* and carries
the same strong metrical emphasis.

398   *Scamander:* pronounce *Skam-and'-er.*
     In Homer an Athenian called Menestheus is said to have

which the chiefs and leaders of the Achaeans
—a great share of the spoils their spears had won—   400
assigned me to be mine utterly and forever,
a choice gift for the sons of Theseus.
From there I have come, speeding onward my unwearied foot,
without the aid of wings, making my billowing aegis rustle,
harnessing this car to young and vigorous steeds.   405
And as I look on this company, new to the land,
I feel no fear, but wonder sits upon my eyes.
Who are you? I address all of you together—
this stranger also who sits here by my image—
you who are like to no race of those begotten,   410
whom the gods see not among the goddesses,
nor are you like the forms of mortals. . . .
But to speak ill of others who are free of blame
is far from Justice, and Right will have none of it.
    CHORUS   You shall learn all briefly, daughter of Zeus;   415

---

fought at Troy. According to a tradition that is later than Homer but was well established before the time of Aeschylus, Demophon and Acamas, the sons of the great legendary Athenian hero Theseus, took part in the campaign. The notion of Athens being awarded part of the Trojan territory at this date might acquire a degree of plausibility from the existence of these stories describing their participation. Yet, it may well have been invented to justify the Athenian claim to Sigeum in the Troad; which had been the subject of a dispute with Lesbos toward the end of the seventh century (Herodotus 5. 94; see D. L. Page, *Sappho and Alcaeus*, Oxford, 1955, p. 152, for details).

402   *Theseus:* pronounce *Thees'-yuse.*

404   The Aegis appears in early Greek art, not as a shield, but as a kind of collar or cloak regularly worn by ATHENE and carrying upon it the face of the Gorgon killed by Perseus. If the text is right, the "steeds" will be the winds, sometimes depicted as or even called horses; "this car" will be the Aegis.

for we are the eternal children of Night,
and Curses is our name in our home below the earth.

ATHENE   Your lineage and the names you are called by I
know.

CHORUS   My privileges also you shall soon learn.

ATHENE   I shall learn them, if a clear account is given.   420

CHORUS   The killers of their kin we drive from their homes.

ATHENE   And what is the limit of the killer's flight?

CHORUS   The place where joy has no existence.

ATHENE   Is that the exile toward which your screeching
would drive him?

CHORUS   Yes; he thought it right to become his mother's
murderer.   425

ATHENE   Was there no other constraint that made him go
in fear of wrath?

CHORUS   Why, what spur is there so keen as to drive to
matricide?

ATHENE   Two parties are present, and we have heard half
the case.

CHORUS   But he will not take an oath, he will not give one!

---

417   In Homer Althaea calls upon the Erinyes to punish her son
Meleager, and we are told that "the gods accomplished her
curses" (*Iliad* 9. 454f). In Aeschylus' *The Seven Against Thebes*,
the curse of a father is identified with the Erinys (70); the
Erinyes were probably first thought of as personified curses.

429   According to a very ancient mode of legal procedure, which
left traces in Athenian law of the fifth century, the accused
was asked to swear that he was innocent, calling upon the gods
to destroy him if he swore falsely. ORESTES could not have

37

ATHENE You wish to be thought to act justly rather than
to do so.　　　　　　　　　　　　　　　　　　　430

CHORUS How so? Explain it; for you are not poor in
wisdom.

ATHENE I say you must not try to win by oaths an unjust
victory.

CHORUS Why, put him to the question, and pronounce
a righteous judgment.

ATHENE Would you commit to me the settlement of the
charge?

CHORUS Surely; we reverence you as worthy and of worthy
parentage.　　　　　　　　　　　　　　　　　435

ATHENE Stranger, what answer do you wish to make in
your turn?
Tell me what are your country and your family and your
fortunes,
and then try to rebut this accusation,
if it is with confidence in justice that you sit
clutching my image near my altar,　　　　　　　440
a suppliant to be revered after Ixion's fashion.

---

denied having killed his mother; and once he had admitted
this, the Erinyes would have regarded their case as won. But
since ORESTES' defense will rest upon a plea of justification,
this request is unfair, as ATHENE points out (430, 432).

441　Ixion: pronounce Ix-eye'-on. The Thessalian hero Ixion was the
first murderer and the first suppliant, and therefore set a prece-
dent. He killed his father-in-law after a dispute over his wife's
dowry, but was purified of the murder by Zeus himself, who even
entertained him on Olympus. Ixion rewarded his hospitality by
making love to Hera. Zeus allowed him to believe he was to en-
joy her favors, but the god substituted a cloud in Hera's likeness;
the result of this union was the Centaurs. Aeschylus dealt with

To all these charges return an answer I can understand!

ORESTES Queen Athene, your last words contain
a great cause of anxiety that I will first remove.
I am no suppliant in need of purifying, nor was it with pollution   445
upon my hand that I took my seat near your image.
And I will tell you of a powerful proof of this.
It is the custom for the killer to be silent,
till by the action of a purifier of blood-guilt
the slaughter of a suckling victim shall have shed blood upon
  him.   450
Long since I have been thus purified at other
houses, both by victims and by flowing streams.
This cause for anxiety I thus dispel;
and what is my lineage you shall soon know.
I am an Argive; and my father you know well,   455
Agamemnon, who marshaled the men of the fleet,
with whom you made Ilium's city a city no more.
He perished by no honorable death, when he came
home; my black-hearted mother
slew him, when she had wrapped him   460
in a crafty snare, one that bore witness to his murder in the
  bath.
And I returned, having been before in exile,
and killed my mother—I will not deny it—
exacting the penalty of death in return for my dear father.
And together with me Loxias is answerable;   465
for he warned me of pains that would pierce my heart,
if I should fail to act against those who bore the guilt of this.
Whether I acted justly or unjustly, you decide the case!
For however I may fare, I shall rest content with your decision.

---

this subject in a trilogy, of which we have only small fragments. In view of the light which this work might throw on
Aeschylus' conception of Zeus, its loss is greatly to be regretted.

452 River water as well as pigs' blood was used in purification.

ATHENE   The matter is harder than any mortal thinks   470
to judge of; it is not right even for me
to decide a trial for murder that brings down fierce wrath;
all the more since, disciplined as you have been,
you have come a suppliant pure and harmless to my house,
and in spite of all, the city has no reproach against you, and I
     adopt you.   475

     Turning to the CHORUS.

But these have an office that cannot lightly be dismissed,
and if they are cheated of victory in this matter . . .
in time to come their anger will drop venom
that will fall upon the ground and become an unbearable,
     grievous pestilence.
So stands the case; either course, that you should stay   480
or that I should send you away is disastrous, and perplexes me.
But since this matter has devolved on me . . .
                . . . . . .
judges . . . of murder, respecting the covenant
of their oaths, which I shall establish for all time.
Do you summon witnesses and proofs,   485
sworn evidence to assist justice.
I will select the best among my citizens,
and will return, to decide this issue in all sincerity.

     All leave the stage, except the CHORUS.

---

482   The number of lines that are missing is uncertain. ATHENE
      now announces her intention of founding a new court to sit
      upon the Hill of Ares and try the case. In 483 the text is
      uncertain, all the more so because we do not know what came
      before it. A line that runs, "never transgressing their oaths,
      so as to do injustice" (?), and which appears after 488, where
      it makes no possible sense, probably belongs somewhere in
      the gap after 482.

STROPHE 1

Chorus Now is the ruin of the new   490
covenant, if the injurious plea
of this killer of his mother
is to prevail!
All mortals from now on will this act
knit fast to readiness of hand;   495
and many the wounds, dealt in truth
by their children, that await parents
yet again in time to come.

For from us who keep watch on mortals
and send madness shall no wrath   500
at these their deeds come upon them;
I shall let loose doom in every form.

ANTISTROPHE 1

And one shall ask of another, while he proclaims
his neighbors' ills,
when shall tribulation subside and cease;   505
and in vain does the poor wretch
offer as consolation cures that are not sure.

---

490 The first two strophic pairs in the Second Stasimon (490–525) are in a trochaic meter similar to that of the first strophic pair in the First Stasimon. The third strophe opens in the same meter (526–29 ~ 538–40); then comes a run of dactyls, recalling those of the second and third stropic pairs in the First Stasimon (530–35 ~ 541–46); finally there is a concluding period in iambics that recalls the iambics of the fourth strophic pair in the First Stasimon. Meter, as well as sense throughout, serves to link the First and Second Stasimon.

490– the new covenant: the institution of the Areopagus; 483–84 496 above are echoed.

STROPHE 2

And let no man call out,
smitten by disaster,
voicing these words: 510
"O Justice!
O thrones of the Erinyes!"
Thus, I think, shall a father
or a mother newly smitten
make lament, because
the house of Justice is falling.   515

ANTISTROPHE 2

There is a place where what is terrible is good
and must abide, seated there
to keep watch upon men's minds;
it is good for them   520
to learn wisdom under constraint.
And what city or what man
that in the light of the heart
fostered no dread could have the same
reverence for Justice?   525

---

517   This passage, in which the Erinyes solemnly insist upon the
good done to mankind by the execution of their duties, is
later echoed closely by ATHENE in her charge to the Court of
Areopagus (681f, especially 696–99). The stress here laid on
the necessity of punishment is wholly in harmony with the
law of Zeus as it is described in the Hymn to Zeus in the
Parodos of *Agamemnon* (160f).

520   Compare *Agam.* 180–81: "Wisdom comes to men against their
will; and the gods who sit upon the august bench of the ruler
give a grace that comes by violence."

521   The text here is uncertain, but the general sense is fortunately
not in doubt. Like the strophe (516), the antistrophe ends
with the name of Justice (Dike).

42

STROPHE 3

Neither a life of anarchy
nor a life under a despot
should you praise.
To all that lies in the middle has a god given excellence,   530
but he surveys different realms in different ways.
I utter a word to fit the case:
impiety's child, in all truth, is insolence;
but from the good health   535
of the mind comes what is dear to all—
that which is much prayed for—happiness.

ANTISTROPHE 3

In all things, I tell you,
must you reverence the altar of Justice.
Dishonor it not,   540
at a glimpse of profit kicking it with impious foot;

---

526   In this context the sense of these words must be that Zeus
      governs the universe, including the world of men, in a way
      that is neither lawless nor dictatorial; he steers a middle course
      between these extremes, delegating different responsibilities to
      different agents. Among these agents are the Erinyes, who
      play an important part in the administration of his law of
      justice.

533   Lack of reverence for the gods and for the divine law leads to
      the brutal insolence (*hybris*) that brings a man or his
      descendants to disaster; we recognize the doctrine whose
      fullest statement is at *Agam.* 750–81. Note in particular how
      one impious deed is said to "beget" others in its own likeness
      (*Agam.* 758–62) and how old *hybris* is said to give birth to
      new *hybris* (*Agam.* 763f).

534   For the content, compare *Agam.* 761–62; the descendants of
      the righteous enjoy prosperity. For the metaphor of physical
      health, compare *Agam.* 1001f.

43

for a penalty shall be exacted;
a sovereign power awaits you.
In face of this, let a man rightly put first the respect he owes
    his parents,   545
and let him reverence
the freedom of the house
whereby a guest and host honor each other.

STROPHE 4

And so without constraint shall he be just   550
and shall not lack for happiness;
and he shall never come to utter ruin.
But he who dares transgress in bold defiance
heaping all things together and carrying them off unjustly
by violence, he, I say, in time shall strike   555
his sail, when the storm of trouble comes upon him
and his yardarm splinters.

ANTISTROPHE 4

And those he calls on shall not hear him as he struggles
in vain amid the whirling waters;
the god's laughter mocks the reckless man,   560
as he sees him, who thought that this should never be,
now enfeebled by irresistible sorrows and failing to round the
    point.
He has run aground on the reef of Justice
the vessel of his former happiness;
he is lost forever,
unwept for and unseen.   565

      Enter ATHENE, APOLLO, and ORESTES.

---

553 For the metaphor of a ship compare *Agam.* 1005f; there too
the offender is said to strike a hidden reef (1006; *Eum.* 564).

ATHENE Make proclamation, herald, and bid the people to
  their places!
And let the shrill Tyrrhenian trumpet
filled with human breath
show to the people its high-pitched note!
For as this court is filled,   570
it is proper that silence be kept, and that my ordinances be
  learned
both by the whole city for time everlasting

---

566 The scene includes ATHENE, the presiding judge; ORESTES, the
  defendant; APOLLO, his advocate; and the CHORUS, who are the
  prosecutors. The Areopagites, who form the jury, and probably a number of other mutes designed to represent the
  audience must also be present. How many Areopagites appeared is not stated; the number must be even, since the
  judge will give a deciding vote, and twelve (the number of
  an Aeschylean chorus) is a reasonable guess. We may imagine
  ATHENE standing or seated in the center of the stage, APOLLO
  and ORESTES on her right, perhaps nearer to the audience,
  and the Erinyes on her left; most of the CHORUS will have
  been in the orchestra, but the leader of the CHORUS was probably on the stage, facing APOLLO and ORESTES. The scene of
  the trial is the Areopagus, the Hill of Ares, as ATHENE says at
  685. There is no difficulty in supposing that after the Second
  Stasimon, the scene changes from the temple of ATHENE on
  the Acropolis to the Areopagus. The places are not far apart,
  and the technique of early tragedy allowed the poet to treat
  them as though they were still nearer. So in The Persians the
  scene changes from the council chamber to the tomb of
  Darius, and then, probably, to a place near the city gate.
567 Tyrrhenian: pronounce Tirr-een'-ian: the Tyrrhenians were the
  Etruscans, with whom the Greeks had been in contact since
  the eighth century B.C.; they were supposed to be the inventors
  of the trumpet.
571f Something is missing after one of these lines, probably after

45

and by . . .
that just decision be duly made of their case who stand here.

> There is a pause; the herald blows his trumpet,
> the jurors take their places, and other mutes rep-
> resenting the audience appear. APOLLO takes up
> his position near ORESTES.

CHORUS Lord Apollo, exercise your sway over what is your
own!
Declare what share you have in this affair!   575

APOLLO *I have come both to bear witness—for according*
to custom
this man is a suppliant and has sat by the hearth
of my house, and I have cleansed him of blood—
and to plead for him myself; and I am responsible
for his mother's killing.   580

> Turning to ATHENE.

Do you bring on the case,
and decide as you know how to!

---

the latter; supposing only one line is lost, it may have run
"and by the judges and by the advocates."

574 The leader of the CHORUS is in effect telling APOLLO to mind
his own business—a prelude to challenging him to prove his
right to take part in the proceedings.

580– The word translated "bring on" is a technical term used to
581 denote the duty that in historical times fell to the King
Archon. He no doubt inherited the duty of presiding over
the Areopagus, as he did other duties, from the kings who
had ruled Attica in the beginning. It is sometimes inferred
that the absence of an Athenian king from this play is proof
of Aeschylus' antimonarchical sentiment. It suits Aeschylus'
purpose, however, to have the goddess herself preside; no
Athenian, however democratic, ever tried to deny the existence
of Theseus, the most famous legendary king of Athens. He
is mentioned at 402, 686, and 1026; his father Aegeus, at 683.

ATHENE (addressing the CHORUS) *It is for you to speak,*
for I bring on the case.
For the prosecutor should first tell all from the beginning
and should rightly explain the matter.

CHORUS *We are many, but we shall speak briefly;*   585
and you answer speech for speech in turn.
Say first whether you are the killer of your mother!

ORESTES *I killed her; there is no denying that.*

CHORUS *There already is the first of the three falls!*

ORESTES *The enemy over whom you utter this boast is not*
yet down!   590

---

583 It was normal for the prosecutor to speak first and establish his case. But instead of the leader of the CHORUS making a long speech, which would be against the normal technique of Aeschylean tragedy, the Erinyes begin with an interrogation of the defendant; from 587 to 606, this takes the form of stichomythia.

585 This line has led some scholars to think that each member of the CHORUS asked a question in turn. Between 587 and 608 there are eleven speeches by the CHORUS; if these scholars are right, 585–86 would have to be spoken by the Coryphaeus and then one line by each of the other members of the CHORUS. The scene in *Agamemnon* (1348–71) in which each member of the CHORUS speaks two lines while Agamemnon is being murdered might be thought to favor this notion; but there is no positive evidence that Aeschylus here departed from the usual rule that dialogue trimeters of the CHORUS were spoken by the Coryphaeus.

587 For the CHORUS, the mere fact that ORESTES has killed his mother is in itself decisive (cf. 429f with note).

589 In Greek wrestling the loser of three falls lost the bout (compare *Agam.* 171–72 and *The Libation Bearers* 339 for a metaphor derived from this fact). What are the two remaining falls?

47

CHORUS   But you must tell us how you slew her.

ORESTES   I will; with sword in hand I struck her in the throat.

CHORUS   And who persuaded you? On whose counsel did you act?

ORESTES   Upon Apollo's oracles; he is my witness.

CHORUS   Did the prophet instruct you to kill your mother?   595

ORESTES   Yes, and up to this moment I find no fault with what befell.

CHORUS   Well, if the vote lays hold on you, you will soon change your tune.

ORESTES   I have confidence; my father is sending help from his grave.

CHORUS   Put your confidence in corpses, you who have killed your mother!

ORESTES   Yes, for she bore the mark of a double pollution.   600

CHORUS   How so? Explain this to the judges!

ORESTES   In slaying her husband she slew my father.

CHORUS   Well, then, you still live, but she by her death has been freed of guilt.

The CHORUS will also have to prove that the killing was deliberate (hence their questions at 591 and 593); and it is a fair surmise that they will also have to establish that it was unjust. ORESTES admits the deed and says that it was deliberate, but he contends that it was justified. The prosecution insists that matricide must be punished, whatever the extenuating circumstances.

595   The word rendered by "instruct" is one used specifically of the kind of instruction in ritual or in religious matters customarily given by the Delphic Oracle. Its use, therefore, like that of the word "prophet," has an ironic effect.

48

ORESTES But why did you not harry her, while she still
lived?

CHORUS She had not the same blood as the man she killed. 605

ORESTES And have I the same blood as my mother?

CHORUS How else did she nourish you beneath her girdle,
murderer?
Do you disown your mother's dearest blood?

ORESTES You now give your testimony, and expound the
law to me,
Apollo, whether I had Justice with me when I slew her.　　610
For the deed—I did it—I cannot deny;
but pronounce upon this deed of blood, whether you think
I acted justly or unjustly, that I may prove it to the court.

APOLLO I shall say to all of you, to this high tribunal
of Athens, that he acted justly, and as a prophet I shall not
speak falsely.　　615
Never have I spoken on my mantic throne
words touching a man or a woman or a city
which had not been ordained me by Zeus, father of the
Olympians.
I bid you understand how mighty is this righteous plea,
and comply with the design of my father;　　620
for an oath has not greater power than Zeus.

---

609 The word translated by "expound the law" is the same as that
referred to in the note on 595; its use reminds us of APOLLO's
special authority.

616 Compare the words of PYTHIA at 19 above. The dependence
of APOLLO's oracle on Zeus was the received doctrine; we find
it stated in the Homeric Hymn to APOLLO (see note on 1).

621 The oath referred to is presumably the jurors' oath; APOLLO
means that even if the jurors think the Erinyes have right on
their side, they cannot condemn ORESTES in defiance of the
will of Zeus.

CHORUS Was it Zeus, you tell us, gave you this oracle,
to tell Orestes here to avenge his father's murder
and to account nowhere the respect he owed his mother?

APOLLO Yes, for it is not the same—the death of a noble
  man,   625
honored by the Zeus-given scepter,
and by a woman's hands at that, not by martial
far-darting arrows, as of an Amazon,
but even as I shall tell you, Pallas, and you too who sit here
to decide this matter by your vote.   630
When he returned from the campaign, having managed
for the most part well, she received him with kindly . . .
          . . . . . .
as he was stepping from the bath, at its edge
she curtained him with a cloak, and in the maze
of an embroidered robe entangled him and struck him.   635
I have told you how he perished, the man
revered by all, the marshal of the fleet.
I have spoken as I have spoken, that the people may be stung
  to anger,
the people that has the task of deciding this trial.

CHORUS It is the father's fate of which Zeus reckons most,
  by your account;   640
yet he himself bound his aged father, Kronos.

622– The Erinyes evidently find it incredible that Zeus, the cham-
624   pion of justice, should defend a cause which to them seems
      patently unjust.

625   The argument based on the doctrine of the superiority of the
      male over the female, on which APOLLO is thrown back, is
      one that few among the play's original audience are likely to
      have questioned.

628   For the Amazons, see note on 685.

632   Probably not more than one line is missing here; line 633 is
      barely grammatical and may be corrupt, but the general sense
      is clear enough.

641   Kronos: pronounce Kronn'-os.

Does not this argument of yours fit ill with that?
I call upon you judges to witness this!

APOLLO   All-hateful beasts, abominations to the gods,
fetters can be loosed; for such hurt there is a remedy,   645
and abundant means of undoing it.
But when once a man is dead, and the earth
has sucked up his blood, there is no way to raise him up.
For against this my father has furnished no spell,
though all other things he turns up and down   650
and disposes without effort by his might.

CHORUS   Why, mark the manner of your plea for his
        acquittal!
Shall he who has spilt his mother's kindred blood upon the
        ground
then live in Argos in his father's house?
What altars of public worship shall he use?   655
And what sacred water of the phratries shall receive him?

APOLLO   This too I will tell you; mark the truth of what I
        say!

The *argumentum ad hominem* employed by the Erinyes is
calculated to disturb those who think that Aeschylean theology always occupies the loftiest heights of abstract speculation.
According to the usual story, probably first related in Hesiod's
Theogony, Zeus overthrew his father Kronos and imprisoned
him in Tartarus. Later, according to one version, Kronos
(Saturn) was released and allowed to preside over the Isles of
the Blessed. This version of the story is told by Pindar in his
Second Olympian Ode and probably by Aeschylus in the lost
part of his trilogy about Prometheus.

655–   The touch of a polluted person would contaminate the altars,
656   which is why such people were excluded from communal
       worship. It would also contaminate the lustral water used at
       the communal sacrifices of the clan. The word "phratry" (cf.
       frater, the Latin word for brother) denotes a kind of clan
       that in historical times had its own religious services. The
       occurrence of the word in a single passage of Homer, where

51

She who is called the child's mother is not
its begetter, but the nurse of the newly sown conception.
The begetter is the male, and she as a stranger for a stranger   660
preserves the offspring, if no god blights its birth;
and I shall offer you a proof of what I say.
There can be a father without a mother; near at hand
is the witness, the child of Olympian Zeus . . .

. . . . . .

and she was not nurtured in the darkness of the womb,   665
but is such an offspring as no goddess might bear.
And for my part, Pallas, in other things I will do all I can
to make your city and your people great,
just as I sent this man to the hearth of your house

---

its exact significance is uncertain, may have encouraged Aeschylus to suppose that phratries like those of Athens in his own time existed during the heroic age.

659 The word rendered by "begetter" is one whose plural is not uncommonly used to mean "parents." Thus, by a play on words, APOLLO is suggesting that a mother is not in the strict sense a parent. He is not actually denying that the mother nurtures the embryo with her blood, as the leader of the CHORUS has pointed out at 607–8.

663 According to an ancient story, Zeus and Hera challenged each other to produce a child without the help of another parent. Hera produced Hephaestus, the lame god of smiths and craftsmen; Zeus produced ATHENE. According to a story, Hephaestus or Prometheus, the smiths among the gods, split the head of Zeus with a hammer and ATHENE leaped out. The evidence of vase-paintings shows this story to have been well known at Athens in the time of Aeschylus.

664 After this line, probably not more than one line is missing.

667f The offer of a bride is less surprising in the light of fifth-century Athenian legal practice than it would be in our own day. Athenian advocates often seem less concerned to establish the innocence of their client than to show that his acquittal will be in the interest of the people of Athens; by "the

that he might be true for all time 670
and that you might gain him as an ally, goddess,
him and those after him, and that this covenant might abide
    forever
for these men's progeny to revere.

ATHENE *Am I now to tell these in sincerity to give*
their righteous vote, since enough has been said? 675

CHORUS *We for our part have now shot every arrow;*
but I wait to hear how the issue shall be decided.

ATHENE *Well, then, how must I dispose to escape your*
    censure?

APOLLO (addressing the judges) *You have heard what you*
    have heard; in your hearts
respect your oath as you cast your votes, O hosts! 680

ATHENE *Hear now my ordinance, people of Attica,*
you who are trying your first trial for the shedding of blood.
In future time also there shall remain for the people of Aegeus
forever this council of judges.
And this hill of Ares, where the Amazons had their seat 685

---

people" they mean the supporters of the prevailing democratic
constitution.

670 Another reference to the Argive alliance (see 28f with note).

681– According to a well-known story, the Court of Areopagus was
682 first assembled to try Ares for the murder of Poseidon's son
Halirrhothius (cf. note on 360). It is possible that Aeschylus
was the first poet to say that the Court was originally assembled to try ORESTES.

683 *Aegeus:* pronounce *Ee-gyuse* [hard "g"]. Aegeus was a legendary
king of Athens and father of the more famous Theseus.

685 *Ares:* pronounce *Air'-es.*
    The Amazons were the race of warlike women who usually
lived near the River Thermodon in Asia Minor. They were

and pitched their tents, when they came in hatred of Theseus
with an army, and over against the city
raised this new city with high walls—
so they sacrificed to Ares, thus giving a name
to the rock and hill of Ares. In this place shall the awe   690
of the citizens and their inborn dread restrain
injustice, both by day and night alike,
so long as the citizens themselves do not pervert the laws
by means of evil influxes; for by polluting clear water

---

supposed to have marched to Athens to punish Theseus for having helped Heracles carry off the girdle of their queen, Hippolyte. Hippolytus was said to be the son of Theseus either by Hippolyte herself or by another Amazon, Antiope. As daughters of Ares, they would naturally have offered sacrifice to him (688).

687   In early times "the city" did not extend beyond the Acropolis, and even in historical times Athenians used to refer to the Acropolis as "the city."

690   "Where there is fear, there is reverence" was probably already a proverb when it occurred in the pre-Homeric epic called *The Cypria,* a work of the seventh century B.C. From this point on it is necessary to compare ATHENE's words carefully with those uttered by the CHORUS at 517f. There the Erinyes are maintaining that fear plays a necessary part in Zeus's government of the universe. In strikingly similar language, ATHENE is maintaining that fear must play a necessary part in the government of Athens. In the government of the universe, the formidable element is supplied by the Erinyes; in that of Athens, it is to be supplied by the Court of Areopagus.

693f   The word translated as "pervert" is corrupt, and the number of words that would make sense by a comparatively slight emendation is embarrassingly large. Fortunately the corruption does not much matter, because it is clear from the general sense that whatever word stood here had a pejorative sense. But it is by no means clear what is meant by "evil influxes." Those who think Aeschylus sympathized with the re-

with mud you will never find good drinking.   695
Neither anarchy nor tyranny shall the citizens defend and re-
    spect, if they follow my counsel;
and they shall not cast out altogether from the city what is to
    be feared.
For who among mortals that fears nothing is just?
Such is the object of awe that you must justly dread,   700
and so you shall have a bulwark of the land and a protector
of the city such as none of human kind possesses,

---

cent reforms of the Areopagus carried through by Ephialtes
(see Appendix, p. 75) argue that the "evil influxes" must
refer to the functions of which the reformers had deprived the
court. Those who think that Aeschylus regretted the reforms
argue that they referred to the reforms themselves; others hold
that he meant the words to be ambiguous. All three parties
commonly assume that "the laws" in 693 refers to the laws
regulating the composition of the Court of Areopagus. This is
possible but hardly certain. If "the laws" here simply mean
the laws in general, the warning against changing them is presumably connected with the fact that the most important function the Areopagus lost was that of protecting the constitution
by vetoing legislation that might transform its character. To
suppose that "the laws" at 693 simply mean the laws of Athens
as a whole happens to be the simplest and most natural way
of taking it, and I believe this interpretation is correct.

696– Compare 526–29 with 696–97; compare 517–19 with 698–99.
699 In both the government of the universe and of Athens, a
middle course between despotism and anarchy must be taken,
and the element of government that inspires fear must not
be excluded. Zeus is no tyrant; he allows men a measure of
free will, while maintaining the rule of Justice among them.
To secure respect for Justice, he makes use of the Erinyes.
Similarly, Athens is neither a tyranny nor an anarchic state;
the laws must be guarded by an element of the constitution
that can inspire fear, and that element is the Areopagus.

neither among the Scythians nor in the domains of Pelops.
Proof against thoughts of profit is this council,
august, quick to anger, wakeful on behalf   705
of sleepers is the guard-post of the land that I establish.
This long exhortation I have addressed
to my citizens to heed in time to come; but you must rise
and take your ballots and decide the case,
in reverence for your oath. My speech is ended.   710

> CHORUS   But mark well! Our company might prove griev-
> ous for your land.
I advise you in no way to dishonor us.

> APOLLO   And I bid you respect my oracles
and those of Zeus, and do not deprive them of fulfillment.

> CHORUS   You concern yourself with deeds of blood, though
> they are not your portion;   715
no longer shall the oracles that you dispense be pure.

---

703   Scythians: pronounce Sith-ians; Pelops: pronounce Pee'-lops.
The Scythians inhabited what is now South Russia, bordering
on the Black Sea. Like the Spartans, who are the natives of
the Peloponnese alluded to in this passage, they were noted in
ancient times for their eunomia, a quality that included both
having good laws and being willing to abide by them. The
comparison of all people with Scythians and Peloponnesians
shows that ATHENE is here especially concerned with the laws
of Athens and their defense against harmful innovation. It
was precisely the powers enabling the Court of Areopagus to
protect the laws that had been taken from it by the reforms
of Ephialtes. Afterwards, it retained few functions except
that of trying cases of murder. The language of ATHENE's
speech, especially when considered in close conjunction with
that of the CHORUS at 517f, hardly suggests that Aeschylus is
content to have the Areopagus concern itself only with the
repression of homicide and give up its duty of acting as the
guardian of the constitution.

APOLLO Was my father too mistaken in his purposes,
when Ixion, he who was the first to kill, made supplication?

CHORUS You say it! If I do not get justice,
my company shall prove grievous to this land in time to come. 720

APOLLO But among the young gods and the old
you are without honor; the victory shall be mine!

CHORUS Such were your actions in the house of Pheres also!
You persuaded the Fates to make men immortal.

APOLLO Then is it not just to do a kindness to him who
    treats one with respect, 725
especially in his hour of need?

CHORUS It was you who violated the ancient dispensations
and with wine beguiled the primeval goddesses.

APOLLO It is you that shall soon fail to win victory in your
    suit
and shall spew out your venom with no harm to your enemies! 730

---

719 *You say it!:* for the idiom illustrated by these words compare
Matthew 27:11, where Pilate says, "Art thou the King of the
Jews?" and Christ replies, "Thou sayest [it]." The formula is
regularly used by those who wish to assent to what the other
speaker has said without taking responsibility for the statement.

723– APOLLO had received many kindnesses from Admetus, son of
724 Pheres, a Thessalian hero. In return the god persuaded the Fates
to allow Admetus to escape the early death that was his destiny
if another person was willing to die in his place. The sub-
stitute was his wife Alcestis, who was rescued from the clutches
of death by Heracles. The subject is handled in the
Alcestis of Euripides, who does not mention the story that
APOLLO made the Fates drunk (*Eum.* 728); it had also been
treated by Aeschylus' older contemporary Phrynichus in a
play that has not survived.

57

CHORUS   *Since your youth is riding down my venerable age,*
I wait to hear justice given in this case,
being still in doubt whether to visit my anger on the city.

ATHENE   *It is now my office to give final judgment;*
and I shall give my vote to Orestes.   735
For there is no mother who bore me;
and I approve the male in all things, short of accepting
        marriage,
with all my heart, and I belong altogether to my father.
Therefore I shall not give greater weight to the death of a
        woman,
one who slew her husband, the watcher of the house;   740
Orestes is the winner, even should the votes be equal.
Throw out in all speed from the urns the lots,
you among the judges to whom this duty is assigned!

ORESTES   *Phoebus Apollo, how shall the issue be decided?*

---

734   Why does ATHENE announce at this point that if the votes
prove equal she will give her casting vote for acquittal? At
some stage this has to be made clear; if she had done so only
after the counting of the votes, the Erinyes might have been
even more indignant. At the actual trials conducted by the
Areopagus, if the votes were equal the defendant was acquitted
by means of the so-called "vote of ATHENE," which was always on the side of mercy.

736   The reason ATHENE gives for voting for acquittal has always
been embarrassing to those who wish to portray Aeschylus as
an "advanced" thinker. In a case in which the arguments on
both sides seem to carry equal weight, there must be a decision
of some kind; ATHENE must decide for acquittal. Yet, she
cannot risk offending the powerful Erinyes by openly proclaim-
ing that as the sister of APOLLO and the daughter of Zeus, who
inspires his oracles, she is on the side of the younger generation of the gods. Before she can calm the fury of the defeated
Erinyes, she has to use all her persuasive power and back it
with a handsome offer.

CHORUS Black Night, my mother, do you look upon this scene? 745

ORESTES Now I must perish by the noose, or else see the light!

CHORUS So must we fall to ruin, or maintain our honors in time to come.

APOLLO Count fairly, friends, the pebbles now thrown out, respecting justice in the sorting!
In the lack of judgment, great harm may be done; 750
but when judgment is present, a single vote can set right a house.

ATHENE This man stands acquitted on the charge of murder; for the number of the votes is equal!

ORESTES O Pallas, you who have preserved my house, I was deprived of my native land, and it is you 755
who have brought me home! And the Greeks shall say, "The man is once more an Argive, and lives among the possessions of his father, by the grace of Pallas and of Loxias, and of him who determines all things, the third Preserver"; yes, it is he who had regard to the manner of my father's death 760
and has preserved me, in the face of these my mother's advocates.
And for my part, to your country and your people
I swear an oath that in future for all time shall prevail, before departing now for home:

---

760 Zeus, in his aspect as Zeus the Preserver, received the third libation at banquets (see *Agam.* 1386-87 and *The Libation Bearers* 1073 with notes).

764 Compare 289f and 670f for what are apparently allusions to the alliance of Athens and Argos that was in force at the time of the play's first production (see Appendix).

that no ruler of my country shall come here 765
to bear against them the embattled spear!
For I myself, who shall then be in my tomb,
shall visit those that transgress the oath that I now swear
with misfortunes that shall reduce them to perplexity,
making their goings dispirited and their paths ill-omened, 770
so that they repent them of their trouble.
But if all goes well, and if they always honor
this city of Pallas with the spear of allies,
then they shall have more favor from myself.
All hail, both to yourself and to the people of the city! 775
May yours be a grip no enemy can escape,
one that preserves you and brings you victory in war!

CHORUS Ah, you younger gods, the ancient laws

---

767 The belief that a dead hero could influence events on earth
must have been firmly held by Aeschylus' original audience.
It plays an essential part, as we have seen, in the plot of
The Libation Bearers, and it is equally important in other tragedies, such as Sophocles' Oedipus at Colonus and Euripides'
The Heraclidae. But it also played a part in fifth-century history,
as we see from the importance attached by the Spartans to the
recovery of ORESTES' bones from Tegea and by the Athenians
to the recovery of Theseus' bones from Scyros; the latter occurred at a date not far removed from the first production of
the Oresteia.

778 The Erinyes give vent to their indignation at the result of the
trial in two stanzas, both prevailingly dochmiac, although the
first has iambic and trochaic elements and the meter of one
part of the second is uncertain. Each of these stanzas is re-
peated (778–92 ~ 808–22; 837–46 ~ 870–80); each of the four
stanzas is answered by a speech by ATHENE in trimeters, the
speeches being of unequal lengths. After the fourth of these
speeches, the CHORUS for the first time shows interest in the
offer with which ATHENE is trying to soothe their wrath (892).
The question they ask there initiates a stichomythia in which
ATHENE and the Coryphaeus each speak one line at a time.

you have ridden down, and snatched them from my grasp!
I am bereft of honor, unhappy one! And with grievous wrath   780
against this land, alack,
venom, venom in requital for my grief from my heart shall
   I discharge,
a distillation for the land
intolerable; and after that
a canker, blasting leaves and children—Ah, Justice!—   785
speeding over the ground
shall cast upon the land infections that destroy its people.
I lament! What can I do?
I am mocked! Grievous, I say,   790
is the fate of the hapless daughters
of Night, who mourn, robbed of their honor!

   ATHENE   Be ruled by me, and bear it not with grievous
     lamentation!
For you are not defeated, but in equal votes the trial   795
resulted in all truth, bringing you no dishonor.
Why, clear testimony from Zeus was there,

This continues until 902 and contains the actual surrender of the Erinyes. ATHENE answers with a speech indicating what kind of blessings she hopes the Erinyes will confer upon her city. This rounds off the dialogue, affording an easy transition to the Third Stasimon, in which the Erinyes comply with her request.

    The Erinyes echo their own words to APOLLO at 731. The theme of a clash between the two different generations of gods is prominent in this scene. In the ancient world, old age was generally thought to confer a special title to respect (cf. 882f).

780   The word usually rendered by "honor" (timē) and its compounds is less abstract than our word "honor" because it also connotes "status," "rights," "privileges"; a man exiled from his city lost his timē. Achilles' quarrel with Agamemnon (Iliad 1) is provoked by what he regards as the deprivation of timē.

61

and he who had given the oracle himself bore witness,
so that Orestes could escape destruction for his deed,
and shall you spew forth grievous wrath upon this land?　　　800
Take thought, do not be angry, and do not cause
blight, dropping discharges supernatural,
cruel spears that will consume the seed.
For in all justice I promise you shall have
a seat and a cavern in this righteous land,　　　805
sitting on gleaming thrones hard by your altars,
honored by these my citizens.

　　CHORUS　*Ah, you younger gods, the ancient laws*
you have ridden down, and snatched them from my grasp!
I am bereft of honor, unhappy one! And with grievous wrath　810
against this land, alack,
venom, venom, in requital for my grief from my heart shall
　　　I discharge,
a distillation for the land
intolerable; and after that
a canker, blasting leaves and children—Ah, Justice!—　　　815
speeding over the ground
shall cast upon the land infections that destroy its people.
I lament! What can I do?
I am mocked! Grievous, I say,　　　820
is the fate of the hapless daughters
of Night, who mourn, robbed of their honor!

　　ATHENE　You are not dishonored; do not with excessive wrath
blight the land of mortals, goddesses that you are!　　　825
I, for my part, have trust in Zeus, and—why need I speak of
　　it?—

806　Sacred stones used to be polished with oil.

808　The verbatim repetition of the lyric stanza (from 778f) marks
　　the total refusal of the Erinyes, at this stage, even to consider
　　ATHENE's offer.

826–　The threat is made in the most tactful way possible, but its
829　presence in the text must not be ignored. The possession of

I alone among the gods know the keys of the house
wherein is sealed the lightning.
But there is no need of it; let me persuade you,
and do not discharge upon this land the words of an idle
    tongue, 830
so as to cause all things that bear fruit no more to prosper.
Lull to repose the bitter force of your black wave of anger,
since you shall be honored and revered and dwell with me!
As first fruits of this great land
you shall have forever sacrifice in thanks for children 835
and the accomplishment of marriage, and you shall approve
    my words.

    CHORUS *That I should suffer this, alack,*
I with my ancient wisdom, and should dwell in the land,
a thing dishonored and polluted!
I breathe forth fury and utter rage! 840

    They utter a loud cry of lamentation.

What pain comes over my sides, over
my brain? Hear, mother
Night! For from my ancient honors 845

---

the thunder enabled Zeus to overcome the Titans, who
supported his father Kronos, and later to suppress the formidable rebellion of the Giants. That ATHENE alone among the
other gods was allowed by Zeus to borrow it is a familiar
story; she used it, for example, to punish the Greek fleet re-
turning from Troy for the violation of Cassandra by the lesser
Ajax in her own temple (Euripides, *Troades* 8of).

832 In the original the sound of this line marvelously suits the
sense: "*koimā kelainou kȳmatos pīkron menos.*"

834– Like Demeter, the earth-goddess, the Erinyes did receive of-
836 ferings after the birth of children and after marriages; that
chthonic divinities should be prayed to for fertility is not
surprising.

842f The text here is uncertain.

the irresistible cunning of the gods has reft me, making me
count for nothing.

ATHENE   I will bear with you in your anger; for you
    are more ancient than I;
and so far you are indeed wiser.
But to me too Zeus has given good understanding.   850
And if you go to a foreign country,
you shall long for this land: of that I warn you!
For advancing time shall bring greater honor
to these citizens; and you shall have an honored
seat near the house of Erechtheus   855
and what you shall receive from men and from processions of
    women
will be greater than anything that other mortals will give you.
But do you not hurl against my country
incentives to shed blood, harmful to the hearts
of young men, maddening them with a fury not of wine;   860
do not pluck out, as it were, the hearts of fighting cocks
and plant in my citizens a spirit of war,
of civil war, making them bold against each other!
Let there be foreign war, which will come easily enough,
in it shall there be a mighty passion for renown;   865

---

849 Wisdom was traditionally thought to accompany old age.

855 Erechtheus was a legendary king of Athens, who was worshiped as a hero in the Erechtheum on the Acropolis; the
present building replaced a much older shrine destroyed by
the Persians in 480 B.C.

863 The prayer against civil war is significant; at the time of the
reform of the Areopagus by Ephialtes in 461 B.C., three years
before the first production of the *Oresteia*, Athens had been
on the verge of it (see also Appendix).

864– At the time of the first production Athens was at war with
865 Sparta, and an Athenian force may still have been assisting
the Egyptian rebels against Persia.

but I do not esteem battle with the bird within the nest.
Such is the choice I offer you:
to do good and receive good, and in goodly honor
to have a portion in this land most dear to the gods.

CHORUS *That I should suffer this, alack,*   870
I with my ancient wisdom, and should dwell in the land,
a thing dishonored and polluted!
I breathe forth fury and utter rage!

They utter a loud cry of lamentation.

What pain comes over my sides, over   875
my brain? Hear, mother
Night! For from my ancient honors
the irresistible cunning of the gods has reft me, making me
   count for nothing.   880

ATHENE I shall not weary of telling you of the good things
   I offer,
that you may never say that by me, who am younger,
and by the mortals who hold this city, you, an ancient goddess,
were driven off dishonored, an exile from this land.
No! If you revere Persuasion's majesty,   885
the power to charm and soothe that sits upon my tongue,
then you should remain! But if you are unwilling,
you could not justly bring down upon this city
any anger or resentment or harm done to its people.
For it lies open to you to have a holding in this land,   890
of right enjoying an eternal honor.

CHORUS Queen Athene, what seat do you say shall be mine?

---

885 Persuasion (*Peitho*) is an abstraction often personified in
     Greek poetry; she often figures among the minor divinities
     attendant upon Aphrodite.

892 Now for the first time, the Erinyes show themselves willing
     to consider ATHENE's offer.

ATHENE One unscathed by any calamity; and do you accept it!

CHORUS Suppose I do accept; what honor awaits me?

ATHENE Honor such that no house can prosper without you. 895

CHORUS Will you bring it about that I have such power?

ATHENE Yes, for him that reveres you I shall make events to prosper.

CHORUS And will you promise me this for all time?

ATHENE Yes; it lies in my power not to promise what I shall not fulfill.

CHORUS You seem likely to persuade me, and I am shifting from my anger. 900

ATHENE Then you shall dwell in this land and shall acquire new friends.

CHORUS Then what fortune do you bid me invoke upon this land?

ATHENE Such blessings as may gain no evil victory:
And these shall come from the earth and from the waters of
the sea,
and from the sky, and the blasts of the wind 905
shall pass over the land with sun-warmed breezes:

---

899 ATHENE expresses herself with a kind of wry humor.

900 Now at last the Erinyes yield. Their question at 902 draws an answer from ATHENE that supplies an easy transition to the ode of benediction that follows.

903 All the blessings described in this speech and in the ode that follows are consonant with the fact that the Erinyes, like other chthonic deities, were implored to grant fertility to women, crops, and cattle.

and the increase of the earth and of the herds, teeming with
  plenty,
shall not cease as time passes to prosper for the citizens;
and so also shall the seed of mortals be preserved.
And may you more incline to make increase the righteous;
for like a gardener I cherish
and keep far from mourning the race of these just ones.
Such things lie in your power; and as for me, in battle's
glorious contests I shall not abstain
from honoring this city among mankind with victory.   915

    CHORUS   *I will accept a share in the house of Pallas;*
and I will not dishonor a city
that the all-powerful Zeus and Ares
govern as an outpost of the gods,
guardian of the altars of the Greeks
and the delight of the immortals.   920
For the city I make my prayer,
prophesying with kind intent

---

916   Each stanza of the ode of blessing is separated from the next
by marching anapests delivered by ATHENE. The first strophic
pair (916–26~938–48) is partly iambic and partly trochaic;
these two kinds of meter are very like each other, and are often
found together. The second strophic pair (956–67~976–87)
is iambo-trochaic mixed with dactyls; the third begins with a
dactylic line and continues in the catalectic trochaic dimeters
(*lekythia*) that have occurred at several places in the trilogy
(see note on *Agam.* 160).

917   Ares is coupled with Zeus, probably because he is the war god
and not because the Areopagus is named after him.

919   In about 448 Pericles persuaded the Athenians to invite the
other Greek cities to a Panhellenic Congress to restore the tem-
ples burned by the Persians in 480 and to establish the freedom
of the seas and peace. Pericles wished Athens to be thought of
as the "guardian of the altars of the Greeks and the delight of
the immortals."

that in plenty the blessings
that make life prosperous
may be made to burgeon from the earth   925
by the sun's radiant beam.

ATHENE *This in good will toward my citizens*
do I bring about. Mighty and hard to please
are the divinities I make to settle here.
All the affairs of men   930
it is their province to manage.
And he that encounters their anger
does not know from where come the blows that assail his life;
for crimes born from those of long ago
hale him before them, and in silence destruction,   935
loud though he boast,
through their wrath and enmity grind him to nothing.

CHORUS *And may there blow no blast ruinous to trees—*
it is the grace I give of which I tell—
so that no scorching heat that kills the buds of plants
passes the boundary of these domains.
And with dread ruin of the crops   940
let no pestilence come upon them.
May Pan make their flocks prosper
with twofold issue
at the appointed time;   945
and may earth's produce
making rich the land with lucky finds
honor the bounty of the gods!

---

934 crimes born . . . long ago: crimes that men cannot help committing because of the guilt they have inherited from their ancestors—crimes like the sacrifice of Iphigeneia by Agamemnon.

943 Pan had received a state cult at Athens in return for his help during the campaign of Marathon in 490 B.C. He was the god of flocks and herds.

947 The word translated "with lucky finds" is in fact the adjective derived from the name of the god Hermes; he was believed to

ATHENE (addressing the judges) *Do you hear this,*
  guardians of the land,
what things she will ordain?
For great is the power of the Lady Erinys   950
among the immortals and those below the earth
and the fate of men they clearly have power
to decide; to some they bring rejoicing
and to others a life
blinded by tears.   955

CHORUS *But I prohibit the events that kill*
men before their time.
To lovely maidens,
you gods that have the power, grant lives that bring them
       husbands;   960
among you are the Fates,
our sisters by one mother,
deities just in apportionment,
who have a part in every house,
whose might weighs heavily in every season,   965
in your righteous visitations
in every way most honored among the gods!

ATHENE *While for my land they eagerly*
ordain such things
I rejoice; and I cherish Persuasion's eye,   970
for having guided my tongue and lips
when I met their fierce refusal.

---

be responsible for lucky finds. The discovery of a vein of silver at Laurium, in southeast Attica, supplied the Athenians with the money necessary to build the fleet that saved them at Salamis in 480. It was Themistocles who persuaded them to use this "lucky find" for this purpose.

962 On the parentage of Fates and Erinyes, see note on line 321.

970 The goddess of Persuasion is conceived of as helping ATHENE by literally casting a favorable eye upon her.

But Zeus of the assembly prevailed;
and victory attends our rivalry
in good things forever! 975

CHORUS *But may the voice of faction, who has never had*
enough of evil,
never in this city
resound, I pray;
and may the dust not drink the black blood of the citizens 980
and through passion for revenge
speed on the ruin to the city
wrought by murder in return for murder!
But may each give joy to each,
in a spirit of love toward the common weal, 985
and may they hate with one accord,
for many are the sorrows among mortals that this can cure.

ATHENE *Have they a mind to find out*
the path of benediction?
Then from these fearsome faces 990
I see great good for these the citizens.
For if, kind in return for kindness,
you do them ever great honor, both land and city
on the straight path of justice
you shall keep, in every way preeminent. 995

---

973 The expression translated as "Zeus of the assembly" is untranslatable. *Agoraios,* meaning "of the marketplace," is a cult-title under which Zeus was worshiped at several places, including Athens; the adjective might also mean "associated with speech-making," which is the point of its use here.

974– Hesiod in a famous passage near the beginning of his *Works*
975 *and Days* (11f) says there are two kinds of *eris* ("rivalry," "strife"), one of which is good and the other bad; the former promotes peaceful competition for getting work done, and ATHENE is implying that this sort of *eris* pertains especially to herself and her citizens.

976 Again we find a prayer against civil war.

CHORUS   *Hail, hail in your wealth bestowed by fate,*
hail, people of the city,
whose seat is near to Zeus,
dear to the goddess who is dear to you,
gaining wisdom as time passes.   1000
On you that sit beneath the wings of Pallas
her father looks with kindness.

   ATHENE   *Hail to you also!*

   Enter ESCORT of torch-bearers.

But I must go first to reveal
your chambers in the sacred light   1005
given by these who escort you. Go, and as this solemn
sacrifice is done, make speed beneath the earth,
and keep far away what is baneful,
but send what brings advantage,
that the city may triumph!
Lead the way, sons of Cranaus   1010
that hold the city, for these fellow denizens;

1005   The cave where the Erinyes were worshiped was on a slope
of the Acropolis, some way from the Areopagus. It would be
a mistake to argue that the procession must actually have
moved in the direction of this place (see note on 566).

1005–   Some time before these lines are spoken, an extra chorus of
1006   Athenians carrying torches must have appeared to escort the
Eumenides. *The Suppliants* of Aeschylus also has an extra
chorus that appears only in the final scene, if the generally
accepted view that the handmaidens of the Danaids sing part
of the final lyric scene is right.

1010–   *Cranaus*: pronounce *Krann'-ay-us*. Athens is sometimes called
1011   by poets *Kranaa polis*, "the rocky [or 'the rugged'] city," and
this seems to have caused the invention of a legendary ancestor
called *Kranaos*, "the rugged one."

1011   The word translated as "fellow denizens" is the word regularly used at Athens to denote resident aliens, or *"metics"*;

71

and may the spirit of the citizens
be good in return for good!

CHORUS *Hail, hail once more, for again I say it,*
all within the city,   1015
gods and mortals!
Govern the city of Pallas
and reverence me who share your home,
and you shall not find fault
with your fortune in life!   1020

ATHENE   I thank you for the words spoken in these your
    benedictions,
and I will escort you by the light of blazing torches
to your place below, beneath the earth,
with the attendants who guard my image,
as you deserve.   1025

        Addressing the ESCORT.

You shall come to the very eye
Of Theseus' land, O honorable band
of children and women and company of aged ladies

            · · · · · ·
honor them with robes of crimson dye,
and let the blaze of fire rise up,   1030
that this their sojourn, kindly to the land,
may in future time be made manifest in fortune that brings it
    noble men.

---

its corresponding noun is the word translated as "share your
home" at 1018.

1025   Greek and Latin both use the word "eye" metaphorically to
mean the most precious part of anything.

1027   There is probably more than one line missing here.

1028   At the procession in honor of ATHENE at the festival of the
Great Panathenaea, the most important festival of the
Athenian religious year, resident aliens wore crimson cloaks.

72

ESCORT   Go on your way, as is right, mighty ones, jealous
    of honor,
dread children of Night, under our honest escort.
Let your speech be of good omen, people of the land!   1035
Beneath earth's primeval caverns,
with honors and sacrifices and with much reverence.
Let your speech be of good omen, people one and all!
Gracious and propitious to the land   1040
come hither, venerable ones, rejoicing
on your way in the torch the flame devours!
Raise a glad cry, echoing our song!
There shall be peace forever . . .
for the citizens of Pallas; thus have all-seeing Zeus   1045
and Fate come to our aid.
Raise a glad cry in echo of our song!

Presumably, the Erinyes assumed the cloaks during this scene in token of their new status.

1033   The extra chorus of the ESCORT sings two brief strophic pairs, both in predominantly dactylic measures of a kind that were thought appropriate to accompany processions because they conveyed an effect of solemn dignity.

1041   "The Venerable Ones" (*Semnai*), like "The Kindly Ones" (*Eumenides*), was a common euphemistic way of referring to the Erinyes.

1044   The text here is corrupt.

APPENDIX

Only three years before the first production of the *Oresteia*, the Areopagus had been at the center of a fierce political storm that had come near to ending in civil war. At the instigation of the democratic leader Ephialtes, helped by the young Pericles, the Areopagus had been stripped of the special powers that it had held in virtue of its duty to guard the constitution by preventing legislation judged not to be in keeping with its spirit. Violent passions were aroused on both sides, and Ephialtes was soon afterwards assassinated; his murderers went undetected. Several passages in *The Eumenides*, and especially part of the Second Stasimon (517f) and Athene's charge to the Court before the voting (681f), must allude to the special function of the Areopagus in a way that has a bearing on the controversy. Aeschylus is the only author who gives this particular account of its foundation, and he may well have invented it in order to make it part of the subject of his trilogy and hence to give himself the opportunity to comment on what was in 458 a burning issue. But though it is generally agreed that the reform of the Areopagus is relevant to the play, opinions differ widely concerning the poet's attitude toward it. Some think that he wished to praise the recent changes; others that he wished to censure them; others, including the great Hellenist Wilamowitz, have believed that

he alludes to them with a studied ambiguity, being concerned only
to promote the reconciliation of the two conflicting factions.

After his acquittal, Orestes promises that his own city of Argos
will never forget its debt to Athens; this has been generally taken
as an allusion to the alliance with Argos that Athens had contracted
in 461. Ephialtes and Pericles were strongly in favor of this alliance,
which meant that Athens had finally decided to challenge Sparta
for the leadership of Greece by making friends with Sparta's chief
Peloponnesian rival. Most of those who hold that Aeschylus looked
with favor on the Areopagus reforms assume that a poet who
complimented Argos and her alliance must also have sympathized
with the views in domestic politics of those who were responsible
for the Argive connection. But it does not follow that a poet who
makes a polite mention of an ally must necessarily share the attitude in internal matters of those who have promoted the alliance.
Organized political parties in the modern sense did not exist in
ancient Athens, and at this time the case for abandoning the old
friendship with Sparta and contracting one with Argos was strong;
it must have appealed to many Athenians who disagreed with the
policies of its chief advocates but were capable of seeing the strong
arguments in terms of national self-interest that could be urged in
favor of this measure.

Let us now consider the words in which the Erinyes describe
their function in the government of the universe, and which are
later echoed by Athene in her charge to the Areopagus regarding
its function in the government of Athens. The element of terror is
necessary to the well-being of a state; neither anarchy nor despotism
is good; freedom must be tempered by the retention of some institution that has power to punish. As long as the Areopagus is there
to guard the land, waking while others sleep, Athens will have a
bulwark unequalled even by the Scythians and the Spartans, the
two peoples famed beyond others for the excellence of their laws
and for the readiness of their peoples to obey them.

Far from wishing to abolish the prerogatives of the Erinyes,
Athene is anxious to conserve them; so, evidently, does the poet
wish to conserve the functions of the Areopagus. But which of its
functions are in question? After the reforms of Ephialtes, the main
function left to the Areopagus was that of conducting trials for

murder. Those who hold that Aeschylus meant to express his approval of the reforms are constrained to argue that the function to which Athene attaches so much importance is simply that of preventing homicide. This is indeed a highly important function of a civilized state, and one which in the early stages is not achieved without a struggle. When studied carefully, however, Athene's speech seems rather to be concerned with the quality known as *Eunomia*, a word by which the Greeks denoted both the possession of good laws and the willingness of the citizens to observe them. In the universe the Erinyes are not merely the punishers of murder or of a special kind of murder, but the defenders of the universal order, of *Dike*, against any threat of disturbance; in the state of Athens the Areopagus had traditionally been, not merely a court to try murderers, but the protector of the constitution, the authority with power to punish that prevented freedom from turning into anarchy. Definite and conclusive proof is lacking, doubtless because it was not the poet's intention to provide it; one disputed passage that has often been taken to yield it does not do so (690–95; see note). But the concern of Athene with *Eunomia* seems to me to make it likelier than not that Aeschylus looked back with regret on the curtailment of the powers of the dignified institution that he presents with such respect. Not that he meant his play for a political tract aiming to persuade the citizens that the powers of the Areopagus should be restored. Rather, he pronounces a kind of splendid funeral panegyric on the Court in its capacity as guardian of the constitution. Athene solemnly warns her people against civil strife, reminding them that there is no lack of foreign enemies (858f; cf. 976f); the play and trilogy end on a note of peace and reconciliation, as the Erinyes, having assumed their aspect of Eumenides, "The Kindly Ones," bestow every kind of blessing upon the city that has dignified them with new honors.

BIBLIOGRAPHY

No adequate commentary on *The Eumenides* exists in English. A Sidgwick's school edition (Aeschylus, *The Eumenides*. Oxford, 3rd ed., 1902), is useful.

During the Homeric age certain categories of crime were punished by the terrifying powers of the underworld—the Erinyes. Although they primarily avenged crimes committed by offspring against parents, they also punished people who had failed to keep their oaths.

In Aeschylus' play, *The Eumenides,* Apollo purifies Orestes by washing him in pig's blood. This, however, does not free him from the attention of the Erinyes, who flatly reject Apollo's order that they should henceforth leave Orestes alone. As in *Prometheus Bound,* there is a clash between gods who belong to different generations. This conflict ends, not in the defeat of the representatives of the old order, but in a settlement in which their claims are fully recognized. The play that has begun by horrifying its audience with the gruesome appearance and bloodthirsty threats of the Erinyes ends by honoring them, claiming that they are among the great benefactors of mankind. Although the Erinyes lose their victim, they are not defeated or disgraced; they are appeased by the grant of new honors, and the importance of their function is emphasized. The lesson taught in the play is that in the city, as in the universe, anarchy and despotism must both equally be avoided; freedom can survive only if it is balanced by the existence of a force that can punish crime.